THE HUMAN FUTURES SERIES

Barry N. Schwartz and Robert L. Disch,
General Editors

FRED BEST, editor of this volume in the Human Futures series, holds an M.B.A. from the University of California, Berkeley. Currently a consultant specializing in work-leisure-education cycles, he has had first-hand experience in agricultural and construction labor, on factory assembly lines, in business administration and political campaigning. He has also directed several government research projects.

*. . . the economic problem, the struggle for
subsistence, always has been hitherto the primary,
most pressing problem of the human race. If the
economic problem is solved, mankind will be deprived
of its traditional purpose.*

*Will this be of a benefit? If one believes at all in
the real values of life, the prospect at least opens
up the possibility of benefit. Yet I think with dread
of the readjustment of the habits and instincts of the
ordinary man, bred into him for countless generations,
which he may be asked to discard within a few
decades . . . thus for the first time since his creation
man will be faced with his real, his permanent
problem—how to use his freedom from pressing
economic cares, how to occupy his leisure, which
science and compound interest will have won for him,
to live wisely and agreeably and well.*

—John Maynard Keynes

the future of work

EDITED BY *Fred Best*

PRENTICE-HALL, INC. A SPECTRUM BOOK *Englewood Cliffs, N. J.*

Library of Congress Cataloging in Publication Data

BEST, FRED, COMP.
  The future of work.

  (Human futures series) (A Spectrum Book)
  Includes bibliographical references.
  CONTENTS: Mills, C. W. The meanings of work
throughout history.—Maslow, A. A theory of human
motivation: the goals of work.—Mitchell, A. Human
needs and the changing goals of life and work. [etc.]
  1.–Work—Addresses, essays, lectures. I.–Title.
HD4904.B48   301.5′5   73–5961
ISBN 0–13–345942–X
ISBN 0–13–345934–9 (pbk.)

10 9 8 7 6 5 4 3 2 1

PRENTICE-HALL INTERNATIONAL, INC. (*London*)
PRENTICE-HALL OF AUSTRALIA PTY. LTD. (*Sydney*)
PRENTICE-HALL OF CANADA LTD. (*Toronto*)
PRENTICE-HALL OF INDIA PRIVATE LIMITED (*New Delhi*)
PRENTICE-HALL OF JAPAN, INC. (*Tokyo*)

To my good friend Steve Camber

contents

Introduction   **1**

PART ONE: The Evolving Concept of Work   **5**

  1   The Meanings of Work throughout History   **6**
       C. Wright Mills

PART TWO: Human Needs and the Changing Goals of Work   **15**

  2   A Theory of Human Motivation: The Goals of Work   **17**
       Abraham Maslow

  3   Human Needs and the Changing Goals of Life and Work   **32**
       Arnold Mitchell

PART THREE: The Issues of Tomorrow's Work   **45**

  **Section A: Technology and Automation:
            Is Work Disappearing?**   **48**

  4   Work and Technological Priorities:
       A Historical Perspective   **50**
       Robert Heilbroner

  5   Evolution of the Knowledge Worker   **58**
       Peter Drucker

  Section B: Organizations: The Changing Work Environment   **64**

  6   Ad-hocracy: The Coming of Temporary Organizations   **66**
       Alvin Toffler

  7   Organizational Democracy:
       Towards Work by Consent of the Employed   **78**
       Warren Bennis and Philip Slater

Section C: Work and Leisure: Future Free-Time Options   86

8   Future Options for More Free Time   87
    Juanita Kreps and Joseph Spengler

9   Flexible Work Scheduling:
    Beyond the Forty-Hour Impasse   93
    Fred Best

Section D: Work and Education: An Emerging Synthesis   100

10 Learning a Living   103
    Marshall McLuhan

11 The Learning Society:
    Institutions to Integrate Work and Education   114
    Report of the Conference on Educational Priorities

**Section E: The Work-Income Link:
Toward Post-Economic Motivation**   126

12 Guaranteed Income Today:
    An Idea Whose Time Has Come   128
    Paul Samuelson

13 Guaranteed Income Tomorrow:
    Toward Post-Economic Motivation   132
    Robert Theobold

PART FOUR: Some Alternative Futures for Work   139

14 The Future Meanings of Work:
    Some "Surprise-Free" Observations   141
    Herman Kahn and Anthony Wiener

15 Misused Technology: Humanity as a Cog in the Machine   155
    Jacques Ellul

16 The Counter-Culture Thrust: Living Poor with Style   162
    Ernest Callenbach

17 Technology and Utopia   175
    Carolyn Symonds

the future of work

introduction

Today, as in the past, our relationship to work activity is a fundamental determinant of the way we live. Our relation to work has determined and influenced our status, the kind of food available to us, our ability to buy goods, our use of time and leisure, the nature of our family and sexual relations, the state of our mental health, and an endless host of other conditions. To put it succinctly, the importance of work is and has been most pervasive; it determines what we produce, what we consume, how we live, and what type of society we create and perpetuate.

In the future the effects of work activities upon our lives will be equally as important as they are today. But added to this importance will be the dynamics of change. Tomorrow's work will be different and constantly changing. It will not only determine the routines and goals of our lives, but it will also increasingly alter these routines and goals. Indeed, the nature of these changes may be so basic as to cause a historic departure of importance equal to or greater than the Industrial Revolution.

Everywhere we look, the changes of our times and their relevance to work appear to be triggering the sensitivities of all kinds of people. Discussions between father and son about the values and importance of work are common everyday events in many families. Newspapers headline political speeches about "welfare chiselers," who are criticized for not doing their fair share of work. Everyday conversations note the need for shifting human efforts toward "new priorities," such as our inner cities, ecology, and education. Yet college graduates who are specifically trained for work in such fields find that their education does not lead to job opportunities. Women's Liberation groups demand equal occupational opportunities and socioeconomic parity for housework. Many of today's youth and growing numbers of adults attempt to "drop-out" in order to escape the "daily humdrum of the work routine." At the same time, businessmen talk with concern about declining work discipline and performance. Questions and discontents phrased in different words and based on different perspectives, are growing in the minds of increasing numbers of people. Many signs point to a steadily emerging societywide debate on the future of work.

This anthology addresses itself to some of the major issues concerning the evolving nature of work within advanced technological and affluent societies. It is important to realize that the future of work is more than a matter of work hours, occupational projections, and income levels. Ultimately, it is a matter of how men and women of the future will seek to define and express their existence. In this sense the future of work is an important question for us all. For as the opportunities and choices of our times expand at ever-increasing rates, we find ourselves increasingly forced to ask fundamental questions. What are we? What do we really need? For what goals should we work? What is the meaning of work?

Throughout most of history the reason for work has been simple—men and women worked to survive. Work was seen as an unquestioned necessity. Parents, teachers, and wise elders of the past cautioned the young that the two most important decisions of their lives would be who they would marry and what type of work they would pursue. The yoke of work was accepted by most with fatalistic resignation. In turn, a chosen field of work gave form and meaning to the lives of most people.

But people have labored for reasons other than necessity. Leonardo da Vinci and Marie Curie are graphic examples of those who have worked for purposes beyond their immediate survival. They suggest some possibilities for the goals and conditions of work in the future.

Ultimately, the evolving goals and nature of work must be seen within the context of human existence itself. For work is purposeful *human* activity directed toward the satisfaction of *human* needs and desires. During the past few years there has been considerable discussion about the revolutionary effects of technology and automation upon work. Without a doubt, the advance of technology is a critical determinant of the evolving nature of work. Yet, despite the tremendous effects of technology, it is not the sole determinant of our futures. While technology may decide inertia, constraints, and opportunities, work is still a human activity, and it will be the actions stemming from our individual and aggregate human needs which ultimately determine the use of technology and the future of work.

It is becoming increasingly obvious today that human needs are not limited exclusively to the acquisition of material wealth. We are not the one-dimensional "economic men" that classical economists envisioned. Rather, contemporary psychology is showing us that we have strong and complex "higher needs" toward social belongingness, self-esteem, and personal growth. We have needs for self-expression, the satisfaction of our curiosity, and the pursuit of beauty and balance. As technology and stored affluence enlarge the options of human choice, it is likely that we will use those options to pursue the satisfaction of these nonmaterial higher needs rather than to continue the production and acquisition of traditional economic wealth.

The transition of work as productive human activity from material to nonmaterial goals promises changes in the work of the future which are of far greater significance than the simple development of a "service economy." As larger and larger portions of our population move toward basic security and affluence, we can expect not only a widespread tendency to give up additional material goods in favor of nonmaterial goals but also a desire to integrate and balance our lives. Whether we call this orientation the pursuit of "quality of life," "self-actualization," or by any of a number of other labels, the net effect will be a growing effort to avoid the compartmentalization of our lives evidenced by today's dichotomy between work and free time. As our social, self-esteem, and growth needs become more important to us, we will be less likely to endure interpersonal alienation, repression of our individual dignity, and the absence of growth opportunities in our work situations. In a nutshell, it seems highly probable that this increasing priority of higher needs will change the products of our work efforts—and the conditions of work as well. Undoubtedly we can expect strong efforts to make the activity of work itself a positive and valued part of the human experience.

Predicting the future in any area is a hazardous undertaking. There are countless determining factors, many of which are yet undefined, and the future of work covers a scope almost as wide as the future of humanity itself. It is doubtful that any volume, no matter how large, could adequately discuss all the contingencies. Certainly an anthology of this length cannot offer a definitive study and conclusion. Nevertheless, some of the most essential issues have been emphasized to provide a basic framework for viewing the possibilities of work's evolving nature.

It is the contention of this book that work's evolution will be determined by the priorities of human needs as they are felt and acted upon within the constraints and opportunities of the times. Part One presents an essay by C. Wright Mills which briefly reviews the evolutionary history of work. Part Two seeks to define human needs as the goals of work and evaluate changing need priorities under conditions of affluence. Part Three provides speculations about the specific daily conditions and goals of work in the future, touching upon the issues of technology and jobs, organizational conditions, work and leisure, education, and income. The fourth and final part presents four overall visions of alternative possible conditions of work in the future.

At root, this book is based upon the belief that human motivations range far beyond the drive for satisfaction of essential and discretionary materialistic needs. It is assumed that there are higher needs which must be satisfied in order to approach the fullest potentials of human existence. The predictions of this volume are based upon a faith in our human need to seek fulfillment of our total capacities through the activity of work.

the evolving concept of work

In discussions about work and the future it is tempting to throw up our arms and exclaim that work is a peculiar human curse, a continual responsibility that will always be with us. The idea that work will always be a component of human existence is a realistic conclusion. However, we must be wary that this conclusion does not lead us to believe that the nature and meaning of work will never change. Quite the contrary, the human work experience has not only changed in fundamental ways since the dawn of history but has tended to change with ever-increasing swiftness as history has unfolded.

To state a truism, the future begins where history ends. With this thought in mind, it is appropriate to begin this anthology with a brief summary of the evolving nature and meaning of work throughout history. The first selection by sociologist C. Wright Mills provides a capsulized view of how the activity of work has changed in the past and sets the scene for the changes we can expect in the future.

Chapter 1

the meanings of work
throughout history

C. Wright Mills

Work may be a mere source of livelihood, or the most significant part of one's inner life; it may be experienced as expiation, or as exuberant expression of self; as bounden duty, or as the development of man's universal nature. Neither love nor hatred of work is inherent in man, or inherent in any given line of work. For work has no intrinsic meaning.

No adequate history of the meanings of work has been written. One can, however, trace the influences of various philosophies of work, which have filtered down to modern workers and which deeply modify their work as well as their leisure.

To the ancient Greeks, in whose society mechanical labor was done by slaves, work brutalized the mind, made man unfit for the practice of virtue.[1] It was a necessary material evil, which the elite, in their search for changeless vision, should avoid. The Hebrews also looked upon work as "painful drudgery," to which, they added, man is condemned by sin. In so far as work atoned for sin, however, it was worth while, yet Ecclesiastes, for example, asserts that "The labor of man does not satisfy the soul." Later, Rabbinism dignified work somewhat, viewing it as worthy exercise rather than scourge of the soul, but still said that the kingdom to come would be a kingdom of blessed idleness.

In primitive Christianity, work was seen as punishment for sin but also as serving the ulterior ends of charity, health of body and soul, warding off the evil thoughts of idleness. But work, being of

"The Meanings of Work throughout History" (editor's title). From C. Wright Mills, *White Collar: The American Middle Class* (New York: Oxford University Press, 1951), pp. 215–23. Reprinted by permission of the publisher.

[1] In this historical sketch of philosophies of work I have drawn upon Adriano Tilgher's *Work: What It Has Meant to Men through the Ages* (New York: Harcourt, Brace, 1930).

this world, was of no worth in itself. St. Augustine, when pressed by organizational problems of the church, carried the issue further: for monks, work is obligatory, although it should alternate with prayer, and should engage them only enough to supply the real needs of the establishment. The church fathers placed pure meditation on divine matters above even the intellectual work of reading and copying in the monastery. The heretical sects that roved around Europe from the eleventh to the fourteenth century demanded work of man, but again for an ulterior reason: work, being painful and humiliating, should be pursued zealously as a "scourge for the pride of the flesh."

With Luther, work was first established in the modern mind as "the base and key to life." While continuing to say that work is natural to fallen man, Luther, echoing Paul, added that all who can work should do so. Idleness is an unnatural and evil evasion. To maintain oneself by work is a way of serving God. With this, the great split between religious piety and worldly activity is resolved; profession becomes "calling," and work is valued as a religious path to salvation.

Calvin's idea of predestination, far from leading in practice to idle apathy, prodded man further into the rhythm of modern work. It was necessary to act in the world rationally and methodically and continuously and hard, as if one were certain of being among those elected. It is God's will that everyone must work, but it is not God's will that one should lust after the fruits even of one's own labor; they must be reinvested to allow and to spur still more labor. Not contemplation, but strong-willed, austere, untiring work, based on religious conviction, will ease guilt and lead to the good and pious life.

The "this-worldly asceticism" of early Protestantism placed a premium upon and justified the styles of conduct and feeling required in its agents by modern capitalism. The Protestant sects encouraged and justified the social development of a type of man capable of ceaseless, methodical labor. The psychology of the religious man and of the economic man thus coincided, as Max Weber has shown, and at their point of coincidence the sober bourgeois entrepreneur lived in and through his work.

Locke's notion that labor was the origin of individual ownership and the source of all economic value, as elaborated by Adam Smith, became a keystone of the liberal economic system: work was now a controlling factor in the wealth of nations, but it was a soulless business, a harsh justification for the toiling grind of nineteenth-

century populations, and for the economic man, who was motivated
in work by the money he earned.

But there was another concept of work which evolved in the
Renaissance; some men of that exuberant time saw work as a spur
rather than a drag on man's development as man. By his own activity, man could accomplish anything; through work, man became
creator. How better could he fill his hours? Leonardo da Vinci re-
joiced in creative labor; Bruno glorified work as an arm against
adversity and a tool of conquest.

During the nineteenth century there began to be reactions
against the Utilitarian meaning assigned to work by classical economics, reactions that drew upon this Renaissance exuberance. Men,
such as Tolstoy, Carlyle, Ruskin, and William Morris, turned backward; others, such as Marx and Engels, looked forward. But both
groups drew upon the Renaissance view of man as tool user. The
division of labor and the distribution of its product, as well as the
intrinsic meaning of work as purposive human activity, are at issue
in these nineteenth-century speculations. Ruskin's ideal, set against
the capitalist organization of work, rested on a pre-capitalist society
of free artisans whose work is at once a necessity for livelihood and
an act of art that brings inner calm. He glorified what he supposed
was in the work of the medieval artisan; he believed that the total
product of work should go to the worker. Profit on capital is an
injustice and, moreover, to strive for profit for its own sake blights
the soul and puts man into a frenzy.

In Marx we encounter a full-scale analysis of the meaning of
work in human development as well as of the distortions of this
development in capitalist society. Here the essence of the human
being rests upon his work: "What [individuals] . . . are . . . coin-
cides with their production, both with *what* they produce and with
how they produce. The nature of individuals thus depends on the
material conditions determining their production." Capitalist production, thought Marx, who accepted the humanist ideal of classic
German idealism of the all-round personality, has twisted men into
alien and specialized animal-like and depersonalized creatures.

Historically, most views of work have ascribed to it an extrinsic
meaning. R. H. Tawney refers to "the distinction made by the
philosophers of classical antiquity between liberal and servile occupations, the medieval insistence that riches exist for man, not man
for riches, Ruskin's famous outburst, 'there is no wealth but life,' the
argument of the Socialist who urges that production should be or-

ganized for service, not for profit, are but different attempts to emphasize the instrumental character of economic activities by reference to an ideal which is held to express the true nature of man." But there are also those who ascribe to work an intrinsic worth. All philosophies of work may be divided into these two views, although in a curious way Carlyle managed to combine the two.

i. The various forms of Protestantism, which (along with classical economics) have been the most influential doctrines in modern times, see work activity as ulterior to religious sanctions; gratifications from work are not intrinsic to the activity and experience, but are religious rewards. By work one gains a religious status and assures oneself of being among the elect. If work is compulsive it is due to the painful guilt that arises when one does not work.

ii. The Renaissance view of work, which sees it as intrinsically meaningful, is centered in the technical craftsmanship—the manual and mental operations—of the work process itself; it sees the reasons for work in the work itself and not in any ulterior realm or consequence. Not income, not way of salvation, not status, not power over other people, but the technical processes themselves are gratifying.

Neither of these views, however—the secularized gospel of work as compulsion, nor the humanist view of work as craftsmanship—now has great influence among modern populations. For most employees, work has a generally unpleasant quality. If there is little Calvinist compulsion to work among propertyless factory workers and file clerks, there is also little Renaissance exuberance in the work of the insurance clerk, freight handler, or department-store saleslady. If the shoe salesman or the textile executive gives little thought to the religious meaning of his labor, certainly few telephone operators or receptionists or schoolteachers experience from their work any Ruskinesque inner calm. Such joy as creative work may carry is more and more limited to a small minority. For the white-collar masses, as for wage earners generally, work seems to serve neither God nor whatever they may experience as divine in themselves. In them there is no taut will-to-work, and few positive gratifications from their daily round.

The gospel of work has been central to the historic tradition of America, to its image of itself, and to the images the rest of the world has of America. The crisis and decline of that gospel are of wide and deep meaning. On every hand, we hear, in the words of Wade Shortleff for example, that "the aggressiveness and enthusiasm which marked other generations is withering, and in its stead we find the philosophy that attaining and holding a job is not a challenge but a necessary evil. When work becomes just work, activity undertaken only for reason of subsistence, the spirit which fired our nation to its present greatness has died to a spark. An ominous apathy cloaks the smoldering discontent and restlessness of the management men of tomorrow."

To understand the significance of this gospel and its decline, we must understand the very spirit of twentieth-century America. That the historical work ethic of the old middle-class entrepreneurs has not deeply gripped the people of the new society is one of the most crucial psychological implications of the structural decline of the old middle classes. The new middle class, despite the old middle-class origin of many of its members, has never been deeply involved in the older work ethic, and on this point has been from the beginning non-bourgeois in mentality.

At the same time, the second historically important model of meaningful work and gratification—craftsmanship—has never belonged to the new middle classes, either by tradition or by the nature of their work. Nevertheless, the model of craftsmanship lies, however vaguely, back of most serious studies of worker dissatisfaction today, of most positive statements of worker gratification, from Ruskin and Tolstoy to Bergson and Sorel. Therefore, it is worth considering in some detail, in order that we may then gauge in just what respects its realization is impossible for the modern white-collar worker.

THE IDEAL OF CRAFTSMANSHIP

Craftsmanship as a fully idealized model of work gratification involves six major features: There is no ulterior motive in work other than the product being made and the processes of its creation. The details of daily work are meaningful because they are not detached in the worker's mind from the product of the work. The worker is free to control his own working action. The craftsman is thus able to learn from his work; and to use and develop his capacities and skills in its prosecution. There is no split of work and play, or work and culture. The craftsman's way of livelihood determines and infuses his entire mode of living.

I. The hope in good work, William Morris remarked, is hope of product and hope of pleasure in the work itself; the supreme concern, the whole attention, is with the quality of the product and the skill of its making. There is an inner relation between the craftsman and the thing he makes, from the image he first forms of it through its completion, which goes beyond the mere legal relations of property and makes the craftsman's will-to-work spontaneous and even exuberant.

Other motives and results—money or reputation or salvation—are subordinate. It is not essential to the practice of the craft ethic that one necessarily improves one's status either in the religious community or in the community in general. Work gratification is such that a man may live in a kind of quiet passion "for his work alone."

II. In most statements of craftsmanship, there is a confusion between its technical and aesthetic conditions and the legal (property) organization of the worker and the product. What is actually necessary for work-as-craftsmanship, however, is that the tie between the product and the producer be psychologically possible; if the producer does not legally own the product he must own it psychologically in the sense that he knows what goes into it by way of skill, sweat, and material and that his own skill and sweat are visible to him. Of course, if legal conditions are such that the tie between the work and the worker's material advantage is transparent, this is a further gratification, but it is subordinate to that workmanship which would continue of its own will even if not paid for.

The craftsman has an image of the completed product, and even though he does not make it all, he sees the place of his part in the whole, and thus understands the meaning of his exertion in terms of that whole. The satisfaction he has in the result infuses the means of achieving it, and in this way his work is not only meaningful to him but also partakes of the consummatory satisfaction he has in the product. If work, in some of its phases, has the taint of travail and vexation and mechanical drudgery, still the craftsman is carried over these junctures by keen anticipation. He may even gain positive satisfaction from encountering a resistance and conquering it, feeling his work and will as powerfully victorious over the recalcitrance of materials and the malice of things. Indeed, without this resistance he would gain less satisfaction in being finally victorious over that which at first obstinately resists his will.

George Mead has stated this kind of aesthetic experience as involving the power "to catch the enjoyment that belongs to the consummation, the outcome, of an undertaking and to give to the implements, the objects that are instrumental in the undertaking, and to the acts that compose it something of the joy and satisfaction that suffuse its successful accomplishment."

III. The workman is free to begin his work according to his own plan and, during the activity by which it is shaped, he is free to modify its form and the manner of its creation. In both these senses, Henri De Man observed, "plan and performance are one," and the craftsman is master of the activity and of himself in the process. This continual joining of plan and activity brings even more firmly together the consummation of work and its instrumental activities, infusing the latter with the joy of the former. It also means that his sphere of independent action is large and rational to him. He is responsible for its outcome and free to assume that responsibility. His problems and difficulties must be solved by him, in terms of the shape he wants the final outcome to assume.

IV. The craftsman's work is thus a means of developing his skill, as well as a means of developing himself as a man. It is not that self-development is an ulterior goal, but that such development is the cumulative result obtained by devotion to and practice of his skills. As he gives it the quality of his own mind and skill, he is also further developing his own nature; in this simple sense, he lives in and through his work, which confesses and reveals him to the world.

V. In the craftsman pattern there is no split of work and play, of work and culture. If play is supposed to be an activity, exercised for its own sake, having no aim other than gratifying the actor, then work is supposed to be an activity performed to create economic value or for some other ulterior result. Play is something you do to be happily occupied, but if work occupies you happily, it is also play, although it is also serious, just as play is to the child. "Really free work, the work of a composer, for example," Marx once wrote of Fourier's notions of work and play, "is damned serious work, intense strain." The simple self-expression of play and the creation of ulterior value of work are combined in work-as-craftsmanship. The craftsman or artist expresses himself at the same time and in the same act as he creates value. His work is a poem in action. He is at work and at play in the same act.

"Work" and "culture" are not, as Gentile has held, separate spheres, the first dealing with means, the second with ends in themselves; as Tilgher, Sorel, and others have indicated, either work or culture may be an end in itself, a means, or may contain segments of both ends and means. In the craft model of activity, "consumption" and "production" are blended in the same act; active craftsmanship, which is both play and work, is the medium of culture; and for the craftsman there is no split between the worlds of culture and work.

VI. The craftsman's work is the mainspring of the only life he knows; he does not flee from work into a separate sphere of leisure; he brings to his non-working hours the values and qualities developed and employed in his working time. His idle conversation is shop talk; his friends follow the same lines of work as he, and share a kinship of feeling and thought. The leisure William Morris called for was "leisure to think about our work, that faithful daily companion. . . ."

In order to give his work the freshness of creativity, the craftsman must at times open himself up to those influences that only affect us when our attentions are relaxed. Thus for the craftsman, apart from mere animal rest, leisure may occur in such intermittent periods as are necessary for individuality in his work. As he brings to his leisure the capacity and problems of his work, so he brings back into work those sensitivities he would not gain in periods of high, sustained tension necessary for solid work.

"The world of art," wrote Paul Bourget, speaking of America, "requires less self-consciousness—an impulse of life which forgets itself, the alternation of dreamy idleness with fervid execution." The same point is made by Henry James, in his essay on Balzac, who remarks that we have practically lost the faculty of attention, meaning . . . "that unstrenuous, brooding sort of attention required to produce or appreciate works of art." Even rest, which is not so directly connected with work itself as a condition of creativity, is animal rest, made secure and freed from anxiety by virtue of work done —in Tilgher's words, "a sense of peace and calm which flows from all well-regulated, disciplined work done with a quiet and contented mind."

human needs and the changing goals of work

Popular concepts or ideologies of work have changed continually through history in accord with the prevailing priorities of human existence. Work has been seen as a curse on humanity, an investment towards life in the hereafter, and a pragmatic path to secular happiness. In the Western world during most of the twentieth century, work has been conceived primarily in terms of the pursuit of material wealth. This materialistic orientation was the natural result of the prevalent scarcity under past economic conditions and of the historic hope of securing basic necessities and attaining some secular comforts.

Today we are nearing a point of saturation with security and material gain as the guiding motivations of our work efforts. We sense the useless and, not so infrequently, negative value of the products of our work. Many of us find our work dull, routine, and devoid of hope and interest. We seem to be working more than we wish and living lives that are less than they should be, to consume goods and services that we really don't want. For increasing numbers, the activities and goals of today's work conflict with their hopes for a better way of life, which seems possible but ever elusive.

Today the cards are on the table. Those of us fortunate enough to live in advanced industrial societies are approaching an evolutionary juncture which will require new concepts of life and work. We sense the need to find new ways to make the most of our lives within the new opportunities and constraints of our times. There is a widespread and growing desire for new priorities of human life. This desire for a better, more holistic, style of life will ultimately lead to the search for a more integrated sense of work which will fulfill the needs and aspirations of our total existence rather than solely our limited economic concerns. Essentially we must reaffirm the meaning of work as a human activity aimed at the fulfillment of real and total human needs.

The search for a new concept or ideology of work must base itself upon an understanding of total rather than partial human needs. The two selections that follow are based upon the motivational theories of the late Abraham Maslow. Maslow's theories, which are gaining increasing acclaim, provide us with one of the most complete models of overall human needs. The first selection by Maslow himself provides a theory of total human needs, then discusses the importance of integrating our need-satisfying efforts into balanced lives and what he calls "synergic" work conditions. The next selection by economist Arnold Mitchell evaluates the relevance of Maslow's need theory in terms of emerging values and work conditions within affluent societies. These selections focus the basic theme of this anthology: As human beings, we have important needs that extend far beyond the mere satisfaction of our material wants, and truly humane work must integrate these needs in a way which gives our lives balance, completeness, and purpose. In sum, it is the totality of our human needs which will guide and shape the evolving goals and conditions of work in the future.

Chapter 2

a theory of human motivation:
the goals of work

Abraham Maslow

I: DEFINING HUMAN NEEDS

Most of what we know of human motivation comes not from psychologists but from psychotherapists treating patients. These patients are a great source of error as well as of useful data, for they obviously constitute a poor sample of the population. The motivational life of neurotic sufferers should, even in principle, be rejected as a paradigm for healthy motivation. Health is not simply the absence of disease or even the opposite of it. Any theory of motivation that is worthy of attention must deal with the highest capacities of the healthy and strong man as well as with the defensive maneuvers of crippled spirits. The most important concerns of the greatest and finest people in human history must all be encompassed and explained.

This understanding we shall never get from sick people alone. We must turn our attention to healthy men as well. Motivation theorists must become more positive in their orientation. . . .

This chapter is an attempt to formulate a positive theory of motivation . . . and at the same time conform to the known facts, clinical and observational as well as experimental. It derives most directly, however, from clinical experience. This theory is, I think, in the functionalist tradition of James and Dewey, and is fused with the holism of Wertheimer, Goldstein, and Gestalt psychology, and with the dynamicism of Freud, Fromm, Horney, Reich, Jung, and

Adler. This integration or synthesis may be called a holistic-dynamic theory.

The Basic Needs

The Physiological [Basic Survival] Needs. The needs that are usually taken as the starting point for motivation theory are the so-called physiological drives. Two recent lines of research make it necessary to revise our customary notions about these needs: first, the development of the concept of homeostasis, and second, the finding that appetites (preferential choices among foods) are a fairly efficient indication of actual needs or lacks in the body.

Homeostasis refers to the body's automatic efforts to maintain a constant, normal state of the blood stream. Cannon has described this process for (1) the water content of the blood, (2) salt content, (3) sugar content, (4) protein content, (5) fat content, (6) calcium content, (7) oxygen content, (8) constant hydrogen-ion level (acid-base balance), and (9) constant temperature of the blood. Obviously this list could be extended to include other minerals, the hormones, vitamins, etc. . . .

Undoubtedly these physiological needs are the most prepotent of all needs. What this means specifically is that in the human being who is missing everything in life in an extreme fashion, it is most likely that the major motivation would be the physiological needs rather than any others. A person who is lacking food, safety, love, and esteem would most probably hunger for food more strongly than for anything else.

If all the needs are unsatisfied, and the organism is then dominated by the physiological needs, all other needs may become simply nonexistent or be pushed into the background. It is then fair to characterize the whole organism by saying simply that it is hungry, for consciousness is almost completely preëmpted by hunger. All capacities are put into the service of hunger-satisfaction, and the organization of these capacities is almost entirely determined by the one purpose of satisfying hunger. The receptors and effectors, the intelligence, memory, habits, all may now be defined simply as hunger-gratifying tools. Capacities that are not useful for this purpose lie dormant, or are pushed into the background. The urge to write poetry, the desire to acquire an automobile, the interest in American history, the desire for a new pair of shoes are, in the extreme case, forgotten or become of secondary importance. For the man who is extremely and dangerously hungry, no other interests exist but food. He dreams food, he remembers food, he thinks about food, he emotes only about food, he perceives only food, and he wants only food. The more subtle determinants that ordinarily fuse with the physiological drives in organizing even feeding, drinking, or sexual behavior, may now be so completely overwhelmed as to allow us to speak at this time (but *only* at this time) of pure hunger drive and behavior, with the one unqualified aim of relief.

Another peculiar characteristic of the human organism when it is dominated by a certain need is that the whole philosophy of the future tends also to change. For our chronically and extremely hungry man, Utopia can be defined simply as a place where there is plenty of food. He tends to think that, if only he is guaranteed food for the rest of his life, he will be perfectly happy and will never want anything more. Life itself tends to be defined in terms of eating. Anything else will be defined as unimportant. Freedom, love, community feeling, respect, philosophy, may all be waved aside as fripperies that are useless, since they fail to fill the stomach. Such a man may fairly be said to live by bread alone. . . .

. . . In most of the known societies, chronic extreme hunger of the emergency type is rare, rather than common. In any case, this is still true in the United States. The average American citizen is experiencing appetite rather than hunger when he says, "I am hungry." He is apt to experience sheer life-and-death hunger only by accident and then only a few times through his entire life.

Obviously a good way to obscure the higher motivations, and to get a lopsided view of human capacities and human nature, is to make the organism extremely and chronically hungry or thirsty. Anyone who attempts to make an emergency picture into a typical one, and who will measure all of man's goals and desires by his behavior during extreme physiological deprivation is certainly being blind to many things. It is quite true that man lives by bread alone —when there is no bread. But what happens to man's desires when there *is* plenty of bread and when his belly is chronically filled?

At once other (and higher) needs emerge and these, rather than physiological hungers, dominate the organism. And when these in turn are satisfied, again new (and still higher) needs emerge, and so on. This is what we mean by saying that the basic human needs are organized into a hierarchy of relative prepotency.

One main implication of this phrasing is that gratification becomes as important a concept as deprivation in motivation theory, for it releases the organism from the domination of a relatively more physiological need, permitting thereby the emergence of other more social goals. The physiological needs, along with their partial goals, when chronically gratified cease to exist as active determinants or organizers of behavior. They now exist only in a potential fashion in the sense that they may emerge again to dominate the organism if they are thwarted. But a want that is satisfied is no longer a want. The organism is dominated and its behavior organized only by unsatisfied needs. If hunger is satisfied, it becomes unimportant in the current dynamics of the individual.

This statement is somewhat qualified by a hypothesis to be discussed more fully later, namely, that it is precisely those individuals in whom a certain need has always been satisfied who are best equipped to tolerate deprivation of that need in the future, and that furthermore, those who have been deprived in the past will react differently to current satisfactions than the one who has never been deprived.

The Safety [and Security] Needs. If the physiological needs are relatively well gratified, there then emerges a new set of needs, which we may categorize roughly as the safety needs (security; stability; dependency; protection; freedom from fear, from anxiety and chaos; need for structure, order, law, limits; strength in the protector; and so on). All that has been said to the physiological needs is equally true, although in less degree, of these desires. The organism may equally well be wholly dominated by them. They may serve as the almost exclusive organizers of behavior, recruiting all the capacities of the organism in their service, and we may then fairly describe the whole organism as a safety-seeking mechanism. Again we may say of the receptors, the effectors, of the intellect, and of the other capacities that they are primarily safety-seeking tools. Again, as in the hungry man, we find that the dominating goal is a strong determinant not only of his current world outlook and philosophy but also of his philosophy of the future and of values. Practically everything looks less important than safety and protection (even sometimes the physiological needs, which, being satisfied, are now underestimated). A man in this state, if it is extreme enough and chronic enough, may be characterized as living almost for safety alone. . . .

The healthy and fortunate adult in our culture is largely satisfied in his safety needs. The peaceful, smoothly running, stable, good society ordinarily makes its members feel safe enough from wild animals, extremes of temperature, criminal assault, murder, chaos, tyranny, and so on. Therefore, in a very real sense, he no longer has any safety needs as active motivators. Just as a sated man no longer feels hungry, a safe man no longer feels endangered. . . .

Other broader aspects of the attempt to seek safety and stability in the world are seen in the very common preference for familiar rather than unfamiliar things, or for the known rather than the unknown. The tendency to have some religion or world philosophy that organizes the universe and the men in it into some sort of satisfactorily coherent, meaningful whole is also in part motivated by safety seeking. Here too we may list science and philosophy in general as partially motivated by the safety needs (we shall see later that there are also other motivations to scientific, philosophical, or religious endeavor).

Otherwise the need for safety is seen as an active and dominant mobilizer of the organism's resources only in real emergencies, e.g., war, disease, natural catastrophes, crime waves, societal disorganization, neurosis, brain injury, breakdown of authority, chronically bad situations.

Some neurotic adults in our society are, in many ways, like the unsafe child in their desire for safety, although in the former it takes on a somewhat special appearance. Their reaction is often to unknown, psychological dangers in a world that is perceived to be hostile, overwhelming, and threatening. Such a person behaves as if a great catastrophe were almost always impending, i.e., he is usually responding as if to an emergency. His safety needs often find specific expression in a search for a protector, or a stronger person on whom he may depend, perhaps a Fuehrer.

The neurotic individual may be described with great usefulness as a grown-up person who retains his childhood attitudes toward the world. That is to say, a neurotic adult may be said to behave as if he were actually afraid of a spanking, or of his mother's disapproval, or of being abandoned by his parents, or having his food taken away from him. It is as if his childish attitudes of fear and threat reaction to a dangerous world had gone underground, and untouched by the growing up and learning processes, were now ready to be called out by any stimulus that would make a child feel endangered and threatened. Horney especially has written well about "basic anxiety."

The neurosis in which the search for safety takes its clearest form is in the compulsive-obsessive neurosis. Compulsive-obsessives try frantically to order and stabilize the world so that no unmanageable, unexpected, or unfamiliar dangers will ever appear. They hedge themselves about with all sorts of ceremonials, rules, and formulas so that every possible contingency may be provided for and so that no new contingencies may appear. . . .

The safety needs can become very urgent on the social scene whenever there are real threats to law, to order, to the authority of society. The threat of chaos or of nihilism can be expected in most human beings to produce a regression from any higher needs to the more prepotent safety needs. A common, almost an expectable reaction, is the easier acceptance of dictatorship or of military rule. This tends to be true for all human beings, including healthy ones, since they too will tend to respond to danger with realistic regression to the safety need level, and will prepare to defend themselves. But it seems to be most true of people who are living near the safety line. They are particularly disturbed by threats to authority, to legality, and to the representatives of the law.

The Belongingness and Love Needs. If both the physiological and the safety needs are fairly well gratified, there will emerge the love and affection and belongingness needs, and the whole cycle already described will repeat itself with this new center. Now the person will feel keenly, as never before, the absence of friends, or a sweetheart, or a wife, or children. He will hunger for affectionate relations with people in general, namely, for a place in his group or family, and he will strive with great intensity to achieve this goal. He will want to attain such a place more than anything else in the world and may even forget that once, when he was hungry, he sneered at love as unreal or unnecessary or unimportant. Now he will feel sharply the pangs of loneliness, of ostracism, of rejection, of friendlessness, of rootlessness.

We have very little scientific information about the belon ness need, although this is a common theme in novels, autobio phies, poems, and plays and also in the newer sociological literature. From these we know in a general way the destructive effects on children of moving too often; of disorientation; of the general over-mobility that is forced by industrialization; of being without roots, or of despising one's roots, one's origins, one's group; of being torn from one's home and family, and friends and neighbors; of being a transient or a newcomer rather than a native. We still underplay the deep importance of the neighborhood, of one's territory, of one's clan, of one's own "kind," one's class, one's gang, one's familiar working colleagues. . . .

I believe that the tremendous and rapid increase in T-groups and other personal growth groups and intentional communities may in part be motivated by this unsatisfied hunger for contact, for intimacy, for belongingness and by the need to overcome the widespread feelings of alienation, aloneness, strangeness, and loneliness, which have been worsened by our mobility, by the breakdown of traditional groupings, the scattering of families, the generation gap, the steady urbanization and disappearance of village face-to-faceness, and the resulting shallowness of American friendship. My strong impression is also that *some* proportion of youth rebellion groups —I don't know how many or how much—is motivated by the profound hunger for groupiness, for contact, for real togetherness in the face of a common enemy, *any* enemy that can serve to form an amity group simply by posing an external threat. The same kind of thing was observed in groups of soldiers who were pushed into an unwonted brotherliness and intimacy by their common external danger, and who may stick together throughout a lifetime as a consequence. Any good society must satisfy this need, one way or another, if it is to survive and be healthy.

In our society the thwarting of these needs is the most commonly found core in cases of maladjustment and more severe pathology. Love and affection, as well as their possible expression in sexuality, are generally looked upon with ambivalence and are customarily hedged about with many restrictions and inhibitions. Practically all theorists of psychopathology have stressed thwarting of the love needs as basic in the picture of maladjustment. Many clinical studies have therefore been made of this need, and we know more about it perhaps than any of the other needs except the physiological ones. Suttie has written an excellent analysis of our "taboo on tenderness."

One thing that must be stressed at this point is that love is not synonymous with sex. Sex may be studied as a purely physiological need. Ordinarily sexual behavior is multidetermined, that is to say, determined not only by sexual but also by other needs, chief among which are the love and affection needs. Also not to be overlooked is the fact that the love needs involve both giving *and* receiving love.

The Esteem Needs. All people in our society (with a few pathological exceptions) have a need or desire for a stable, firmly based, usually high evaluation of themselves, for self-respect, or self-esteem, and for the esteem of others. These needs may therefore be classified into two subsidiary sets. These are, first, the desire for strength, for achievement, for adequacy, for mastery and competence, for confidence in the face of the world, and for independence and freedom.[2] Second, we have what we may call the desire for

[2] Whether or not this particular desire is universal we do not know. The crucial question, especially important today, is, Will men who are enslaved and dominated inevitably feel dissatisfied and rebellious? We may assume on the basis of commonly known clinical data that a man who has known true freedom (not paid for by giving up safety and security but rather built on the basis of adequate safety and security) will not willingly or easily allow his freedom to be taken away from him. But we do not know for sure that this is true for the person born into slavery. . . .

reputation or prestige (defining it as respect or esteem from other people), status, fame and glory, dominance, recognition, attention, importance, dignity, or appreciation. . . .

Satisfaction of the self-esteem need leads to feelings of self-confidence, worth, strength, capability, and adequacy, of being useful and necessary in the world. But thwarting of these needs produces feelings of inferiority, of weakness, and of helplessness. These feelings in turn give rise to either basic discouragement or else compensatory or neurotic trends. An appreciation of the necessity of basic self-confidence and an understanding of how helpless people are without it can be easily gained from a study of severe traumatic neurosis.[3]

From the theologians' discussion of pride and *hubris,* from the Frommian theories about the self-perception of untruth to one's own nature, from the Rogerian work with self, from essayists like Ayn Rand, and from other sources as well, we have been learning more and more of the dangers of basing self-esteem on the opinions of others rather than on real capacity, competence, and adequacy to the task. The most stable and therefore most healthy self-esteem is based on *deserved* respect from others rather than on external fame or celebrity and unwarranted adulation. Even here it is helpful to distinguish the actual competence and achievement that is based on sheer will power, determination and responsibility, from that which comes naturally and easily out of one's own true inner nature, one's constitution, one's biological fate or destiny, or as Horney puts it, out of one's Real Self rather than out of the idealized pseudo-self.

The Need for Self-Actualization. Even if all these needs are satisfied, we may still often (if not always) expect that a new discontent and restlessness will soon develop, unless the individual is doing what *he,* individually, is fitted for. A musician must make music, an artist must paint, a poet must write, if he is to be ultimately at peace with himself. What a man *can* be, he *must* be. He must be true to his own nature. This need we may call self-actualization. . . .

This term, first coined by Kurt Goldstein, is being used in this book in a much more specific and limited fashion. It refers to man's desire for self-fulfillment, namely, to the tendency for him to become actualized in what he is potentially. This tendency might be phrased as the desire to become more and more what one idiosyncratically is, to become everything that one is capable of becoming.

[3] For more extensive discussion of normal self-esteem, as well as for reports of various researches, see the bibliography on page 61 [of Maslow, *Motivation and Personality*]. Also see the work of McClelland and his co-workers. . . .

The specific form that these needs will take will of course vary greatly from person to person. In one individual it may take the form of the desire to be an ideal mother, in another it may be expressed athletically, and in still another it may be expressed in painting pictures or in inventions.[4] At this level, individual differences are greatest.

The clear emergence of these needs usually rests upon some prior satisfaction of the physiological, safety, love, and esteem needs.

The Preconditions for the Basic Need Satisfactions. There are certain conditions that are immediate prerequisites for the basic need satisfactions. Danger to these is reacted to as if it were direct danger to the basic needs themselves. Such conditions as freedom to speak, freedom to do what one wishes so long as no harm is done to others, freedom to express oneself, freedom to investigate and seek for information, freedom to defend oneself, justice, fairness, honesty, orderliness in the group are examples of such preconditions for basic need satisfactions. Thwarting in these freedoms will be reacted to with a threat or emergency response. These conditions are not ends in themselves but they are *almost* so since they are so closely related to the basic needs, which are apparently the only ends in themselves. These conditions are defended because without them the basic satisfactions are quite impossible, or at least, severely endangered.

If we remember that the cognitive capacities (perceptual, intellectual, learning) are a set of adjustive tools, which have, among other functions, that of satisfaction of our basic needs, then it is clear that any danger to them, any deprivation or blocking of their free use, must also be indirectly threatening to the basic needs themselves. Such a statement is a partial solution of the general problems of curiosity, the search for knowledge, truth, and wisdom, and the ever-persistent urge to solve the cosmic mysteries. Secrecy, censorship, dishonesty, blocking of communication threaten *all* the basic needs.

We must therefore introduce another hypothesis and speak of degrees of closeness to the basic needs, for we have already pointed

[4] Clearly creative behavior, like painting, is like any other behavior in having multiple determinants. It may be seen in innately creative people whether they are satisfied or not, happy or unhappy, hungry or sated. Also it is clear that creative activity may be compensatory, ameliorative, or purely economic. It is my impression (from informal experiments) that it is possible to distinguish the artistic and intellectual products of basically satisfied people from those of basically unsatisfied people by inspection alone. In any case, here too we must distinguish, in a dynamic fashion, the overt behavior itself from its various motivations or purposes.

out that *any* conscious desires (partial goals) are more or less important as they are more or less close to the basic needs. The same statement may be made for various behavior acts. An act is psychologically important if it contributes directly to satisfaction of basic needs. The less directly it so contributes, or the weaker this contribution is, the less important this act must be conceived to be from the point of view of dynamic psychology. A similar statement may be made for the various defense or coping mechanisms. Some are directly related to the protection or attainment of the basic needs, others are only weakly and distantly related. Indeed, if we wished, we could speak of more basic and less basic defense mechanisms, and then affirm that danger to the more basic defenses is more threatening than danger to less basic defenses (always remembering that this is so only because of their relationship to the basic needs).

II: HUMAN NEEDS AND WORK *

. . . The only happy people I know are the ones who are working well at something they consider important. . . . this [is] universal truth for all my self-actualizing subjects. They [are] metamotivated by meta-needs . . . expressed in their devotion to, dedication to, and identification with some great and important job. This was true for every single case. . . .

. . . S-A [self-actualizing] work transcends the self without trying to, and achieves the kind of loss of self-awareness and self-consciousness that the easterners, the Japanese and Chinese and so on, keep on trying to attain. S-A work is simultaneously a seeking and fulfilling of the self *and* also an achieving of the selflessness which is the ultimate expression of *real* self. It resolves the dichotomy between selfish and unselfish. Also between inner and outer—because the cause for which one works in S-A work is introjected and becomes part of the self so that the world and the self are no longer different. The inner and the outer world fuse and become one and the same. The same is true for the subject-object dichotomy. . . .

If you take into yourself something important from the world, then you yourself become important thereby. You have made yourself important thereby, as important as that which you have intro-

* "Human Needs and Work" (editor's title). Excerpted from Abraham Maslow, *Eupsychian Management* (Homewood, Illinois: Richard D. Irwin, Inc. and The Dorsey Press, 1965), pp. 6–9, 12–13, 88–89, 236–39. Reprinted by permission of Richard D. Irwin, Inc.

jected and assimilated to yourself. At once, it matters if you die, or if you are sick, or if you can't work, etc. Then you must take care of yourself, you must respect yourself, you have to get plenty of rest, not smoke or drink too much, etc. You can no longer commit suicide—that would be too selfish. It would be a loss for the world. You are needed, useful. This is the easiest way to feel needed. Mothers with babies do not commit suicide as easily as nonmothers. People in the concentration camps who had some important mission in life, some duty to live for or some other people to live for tended to stay alive. It was the other ones who gave up and sank into apathy and died without resistance. . . .

. . . If work is introjected into the self (I guess it always is, more or less, even when one tries to prevent it), then the relationship between self-esteem and work is closer than I had thought. Especially healthy and stable self-esteem (the feeling of worth, pride, influence, importance, etc.) rests on good, worthy work to be introjected, thereby becoming part of the self. Maybe more of our contemporary malaise is due to introjection of nonprideful, robotized, broken-down-into-easy-bits kind of work than I had thought. The more I think about it, the more difficult I find it to *conceive* of feeling proud of myself, self-loving and self-respecting, if I were working, for example, in some chewing gum factory, or a phony advertising agency, or in some factory that turned out shoddy furniture. I've written so far of "real achievement" as a basis for solid self-esteem, but I guess this is too general and needs more spelling out. Real achievement means inevitably a worthy and virtuous task. To do some idiotic job very well is certainly *not* real achievement. I like my phrasing, "What is not worth doing is not worth doing well." . . .

Notes on Synergy

Social synergy as used first by Ruth Benedict to apply to the degree of health of the primitive culture she was studying meant essentially that a synergic institution was one that arranged it so that a person pursuing his selfish ends was automatically helping other people thereby; and that a person trying to be altruistic and helping other people and being unselfish, was also automatically and willy-nilly helping along his own selfish advantages. That is to say, it was a resolution of the dichotomy between selfishness and unselfishness, showing very clearly that the opposition of selfishness and unselfishness or their mutual exclusiveness was a function of a poorly developed culture. I have shown this to be true within the individual in about the same way, winding up with the statement that where selfishness and unselfishness are mutually exclusive, this is a sign of mild psychopathology within the individual.

Self-actualizing people rise above the dichotomy between selfishness and unselfishness, and this can be shown in various ways. One is that they get pleasure from the pleasures of other people. That is, they get selfish pleasures from the pleasures of other people, which is a way of saying unselfish. The example that I used a long time ago can serve here—if I get more pleasure out of feeding my strawberries into the mouth of my little beloved child, who loves strawberries, and who smacks her lips over them, and if I thereby have a wonderful time and enjoy myself watching her eat the strawberries, which would certainly give me pleasure if I myself ate them, then what shall I say about the selfishness or the unselfishness of this act? Am I sacrificing something? Am I being altruistic? Am I being selfish, because after all I'm enjoying myself? Obviously, the best way to say this is that the words "selfish" and "unselfish" as opposites, as mutually exclusive, have become meaningless. The two words have fused together. My action is neither selfish exclusively nor unselfish exclusively, or it can be said to be both selfish and unselfish simultaneously. Or, as I prefer the more sophisticated way of saying it, the action is synergic. That is, what is good for my child is good for me, what is good for me is good for the child, what gives the child pleasure gives me pleasure, what gives me pleasure gives the child pleasure, and all the lines of difference fall and we can say now that these two persons are identified and in certain functional theoretical ways have become a single unit. Very often this is so. We learn to treat a loving wife and husband as a single unit; an insult to the one is an insult to the other, shoes on the feet of one make the other's feet feel good, etc., etc.

This happens to be also a pretty decent definition of love, namely, that the two separate sets of needs become fused into a single set of needs for the new unit. Or love exists when the happiness of the other makes me happy, or when I enjoy the self-actualization of the other as much as I do my own, or when the differentiation between the word "other" and the words "my own" has disappeared. Where there is mutual property, where the words change into "we," "us," "ours." Another definition of love is that happiness of the other is the condition of my own happiness. Synergy is the same kind of thing, and it involves a kind of love-identification. One might say it means in certain respects different people can be treated as if they were not different, as if they were one, as if they were pooled, or lumped, or fused into a new kind of unit which was superordinate and included them both, fusing their separateness. . . .

On Low Grumbles, High Grumbles, and Metagrumbles

. . . People can live at various levels in the motivation hierarchy, that is, they can live a high life or a low life, they can live barely at the level of survival in the jungle, or they can live in an eupsychian society with good fortune and with all the basic needs taken care of so that they can live at a higher level and think about the nature of poetry or mathematics or that kind of thing.

There are various ways of judging the motivational level of life. For instance, one can judge the level at which people live by the kind of humor that they laugh at. The person living at the lowest need levels is apt to find hostile and cruel humor very amusing, e.g., the old lady who is getting bitten by a dog or the town moron who is being plagued by the other children, etc. The Abraham Lincoln type of humor—the philosophical, educational type of humor—brings a smile rather than a belly laugh; it has little to do with hostility or conquest. This higher type of humor cannot be understood at all by the person living at the lower need levels. . . .

In the same way it was my thought that the level of complaints —which is to say, the level of what one needs and craves and wishes for—can be an indicator of the motivational level at which the person is living; and if the level of complaints is studied in the industrial situation, it can be used also as a measure of the level of health of the whole organization, especially if one has a large enough sampling.

For instance, take the workers living in the authoritarian jungle industrial situation in which fear and want and even simple starvation are a real possibility, and determine the choice of job and the way in which bosses will behave and the submissiveness with which workers will accept cruelty, etc., etc. Such workers who have complaints or grumbles are apt to be falling short of basic needs which are low in the hierarchy. At this lowest level this means complaints about cold and wet and danger to life and fatigue and poor shelter and all of these basic biological necessities.

Certainly, in the modern industrial situation, if one runs across complaints of this sort, then this is an indication of extremely poor management and an extremely low level of living in the organization. In even average industrial situations, this kind of complaint, this sort of low grumble hardly ever comes up. On the positive side, that is, those complaints which represent a wish or craving out ahead of what is now available—these are at this same low level approximately. That is, the worker in Mexico might be making positive grumbles at the security and safety level, at such things as being fired arbitrarily, of not being able to plan his family budget because he does not know how long the job will last. He may complain about a total lack of job security, about the arbitrariness of the foreman, about the kinds of indignities that he has to take in order to keep his job, etc. I think we can call low grumbles those grumbles which come at the biological and at the safety level, perhaps, also, at the level of gregariousness and belonging to the informal, sociable group.

The higher-need levels would be mostly at the level of esteem and self-esteem, where questions would be involved of dignity, of autonomy, of self-respect, of respect from the other; feelings of worth, of getting praise and rewards and credit for one's accomplishments and the like. Grumbles at this level would probably be mostly about something that involved loss of dignity or the threat to self-esteem or to prestige. Now, so far as the metagrumbles are concerned, what I have in mind here are the metamotivations which hold in the self-actualizing life. . . . These metaneeds for perfection, for justice, for beauty, for truth, and the like also show themselves in the industrial situation where there might very well be complaints about inefficiency (even when this does not affect the pocket of the complainer). In effect, then, he is making a statement about the imperfection of the world in which he lives (again not a selfish complaint but an impersonal and altruistic philosopher's complaint, one might almost call it). Or he might complain about not being given the full truth, all the facts, or about other blocks in the free flow of communications.

This preference for truth and honesty and all the facts again is one of the metaneeds rather than one of the "basic" needs, and people who have the luxury of complaining at this level are strictly living a very high-level life. In the society which is cynical, which is run by thieves or by tyrants or by nasty people, one would get no such complaints as this—the complaints would be at a lower level. Complaints about justice are also metagrumbles, and I see plenty of them in the protocols from the workers in a well-managed place. They are apt to complain about an injustice even where it is to their personal financial advantage. Another kind of metagrumble is the complaint about a virtue not being rewarded, and about villainy getting these rewards, i.e., a failure of justice.

In other words, everything above implies very strongly that human beings will always complain. There is no Garden of Eden, there is no paradise, there is no heaven except for a passing moment or two. Whatever satisfactions are given to human beings, it is inconceivable that they should be perfectly content with these. This in itself would be a negation of the highest reaches of human nature because it would imply that no improvements could be made after this point—and this, of course, is nonsense. We cannot conceive of a million years of further development bringing such a perfection to pass. Human beings will always be able to tuck in under their belts whatever gratifications, whatever blessings, whatever good fortune are available. They'll be absolutely delighted with these blessings for a little while. And then, as soon as they get used to them, they'll forget about them and start reaching out into the future for still higher blessings, as they restlessly perceive how things could be even more perfect than they are at this moment. This looks to me like an eternal process going on into the future forever. . . .

Chapter 3

human needs and the changing
goals of life and work

Arnold Mitchell

In the . . . forecasting study reported here, one type of probe into the future was explored. . . . This study constructs a profile of society in terms of needs and concerns of people and [makes] rough estimates of what fraction of today's Americans operate modally in each of five need levels. The purpose of the present study was to examine some of the ways in which this humanistic view of society could be exploited in examining alternative futures. . . .

. . . There are many possible approaches to study of the future shape of society. The fact that the present work is chiefly a humanistic approach by no means suggests that others are not fully as useful and valid. We elected to pursue the humanistic route because it has been much less explored than economic, demographic, technological, or political routes and because it appealed to us as especially appropriate. . . . Humans, after all, are the ones who must change if society is to change.

BASIC APPROACH

. . . The basic concept underlying the needs-concerns view of society embraces a needs hierarchy comprising five levels. These levels (based on the theories of Abraham Maslow) are seen as describing a natural progression of human growth from childhood to full psychological maturity. In order for growth to take place from one level to another, concern with the first level must diminish (the needs associated with that level must be partially satiated) so that it no

"Human Needs and the Changing Goals of Life and Work" (editor's title). Excerpted from Arnold Mitchell, *Alternative Futures: An Exploration of a Humanistic Approach to Social Forecasting* (Menlo Park, Calif.: Stanford Research Institute, 1967), pp. 2–7, 9–10, 12–13, 27–32, 34–35, 43.

longer defines the [main] concerns of the individual. Only then is he able to "graduate" to the next need level. . . .

As background for understanding the charts and discussion of this report, a brief description of the psychological syndrome associated with each need level is given below. Levels 1 and 2 have been combined for this purpose because they share many attributes. . . .

Level 1: Survival and Level 2: Security

Dominant Value Patterns. Great concern with surviving, being protected, unthreatened, safe. Concern extends through all levels from one's self through family, community, nation, and even the world. Similarly, threats are sensed at every level: physical, economic, emotional, intellectual, spiritual, and so forth.

Many of the world's people are driven by survival and safety concerns. Typically the small-scale farmer or businessman seeks protection from eradication before all else. Some primitive tribes—and all nations and individuals when emergencies threaten life-giving essentials—operate at the survival level. Nations at transitional and early take-off stages of development probably can be characterized as responding modally to safety needs. Advanced nations in times of distress (defeat at war, severe depressions, etc.) may revert to this level. . . .

Typical Psychological Traits. Insecure, fearful, ruled by appetites, little "moral sense," unplanning, single-minded, short interest span, volatile, . . . intense, uncooperative, envious, jealous, distrustful, universe perceived as hostile, dependent, . . . unadventuresome, rigid, seeks familiar, see things in black and white, believes in luck, few social contacts, afraid of new, traditional, status quo orientation, paranoic, little self-confidence, compulsive, believes system is against, wants strong leader, dislikes making decisions, will fight only when cornered, has a little which is not willing to risk to gain a lot, sees life as a zero-sum game.

At the survival and safety levels the better-off world is thought of as a stingy, unrelenting "they."

Typical Origins. Severely deprived or penurious upbringing; extreme poverty; life-long lack of success; minority or other "outsider" background; lack of opportunity to grow; failure to get the "usual" rewards; rewards dispensed by authorities rather than earned; social contacts capricious; world perceived as arbitrary and unstructured.

Typical Groups. Minorities, poor, disenfranchised, avid union members, marginal farmers and small businessmen.

Level 3: Belongingness

Dominant Value Patterns. The preciousness of being part of something bigger produces for the first time the ability to establish stable coalitions. This salient fact induces the dominant value pattern: that of conformity to the group norm, the sense that there is a "right" and a "wrong" way of looking at things, sometimes the conviction that only people who are like oneself are "good."

Nations with highly specificatory or cradle-to-grave governments belong at this level. Similarly, the tendency of residents of the South or of New England not to accept "strangers" partakes of the belongingness need.

Typical Psychological Traits. Conforming, puritanical, matriarchal, mass-oriented, conventional, sentimental, conservative, needs to be popular, xenophobic, safety in numbers, being an "insider," outer-directed, needs praise, leads only in established endeavors, accepts lowest common denominator, closeness quite formalized, gregarious, prefers many acquaintances to a few deep friendships, "should" and "ought" dominant words, system rewards virtue, prefers status quo, nonexperimental, gossipy, stereotyped, dependent on opinion of others, alikeness a virtue, threatened by the aberrant, "togetherness" a way of life.

The world is seen as "we," for there is much to protect, much to cherish, and the group is at stake.

Typical Origins. Lack of warm upbringing; exposed to much rejection or ridicule; conventional mores in family; criticized for unusual ideas; dependency and conformity cultivated through differential reward.

Typical Groups. The organization man; middle class; specialty cults; routine teachers; happy tract dwellers; hero worshippers.

Level 4: Esteem

Dominant Value Patterns. The dominant value at this stage is that of achievement, frequently expressed as visible, even ostentatious, "success."

Esteem needs and values are those of the "typical" American—meaning those of the American power structure.

Typical Psychological Traits. Materialistic, ambitious, power-oriented, status seeking, authoritarian, self-confident, high-pressured, entrepreneurial, possession-conscious, competitive, "better than" syndrome, winner/loser approaach to things, get things done, upwardly mobile, measurement-oriented, active, planning, hardworking, driving, driven, dynastic, manipulative, efficient, hard-nosed, fame- or money-oriented, effective.

The world of the esteemer is an "I" world—one that has much to offer if only the battles can be won.

Typical Origins. Pater familias upbringing; keeping-up-with-Joneses family values; wealth; status-conscious background; rewards given in terms of pay-off; world viewed as a contest arena.

Typical Groups. Business executives; political leaders; college professors; many professional and technical workers; nouveaux riches.

Level 5: Growth

Dominant Value Patterns. The key value pattern is concern with living up to one's inner potential through full expression of what seems important. The self-actualizer is the emotionally mature person able to express himself fully, tapping the full range of his abilities, in the way that is peculiarly his. No nation and very few individuals operate at this mode.

Typical Psychological Traits. Individualistic, expressive, acceptance of self and others, realistic, spontaneous, problem centered, autonomous, unenculturated, inner driven, freshness of appreciation, tempered idealism, universalistic in feelings, democratic, uncensorious, unhostile, creative, sense of awe and mystic, motivated by ends not means, self-reliant, flexible, willing to lead or follow, few but deep friendships, at peace with self, likes unexplored, sense of mission, understands self, permissive, varied interests.

The world as seen by the self-actualizer is an "all" world—not "they," or "we," or "I." It is a world that could be better—much better—but it is good enough to justify all possible effort to improve it.

Typical Origins. An upbringing that reacts to experimentation without censoring, effort with appropriate reward, confusion with explanation, anger with understanding, love with love.

Typical Groups. There are no typical groups, only individuals. They are found in every walk of life, in every occupation, with every type of interest.

The first four levels are seen as "deficiency" states in the sense that the specific and satiable need patterns arise from internal or external lacks or deficiencies. The fifth level (that of "growth" or "self-actualization") is not a deficiency state because the person is not striving to obtain something he does not have but, rather, merely to express himself to his fullest potential. It is perhaps worth noting that an individual's modal concerns can, and do, fluctuate among need levels on a minute-by-minute basis as well as with a much slower rhythm. When we describe a person as representative of level X we mean only that his modal concerns revolve around this need level, not that this level defines him wholly or at every moment of his day.

Since a person changes as he grows from one need level to another, one would expect his values and attitudes to shift, thus influencing the kind of society he would seek to build. Our first effort was therefore to spell out key aspects of the five needs levels. Then, when considering the consequences of changing the modal needs profile of a society, we asked ourselves how might people operating in that needs milieu reasonably be expected to act, react, aspire, think, value—in short, what kind of a society would they tend to create. . . .

OUTLINING ALTERNATIVE POSSIBLE FUTURES

Once the general basis for a needs-concerns view of society was established, [we] selected . . . possible (but not equally probable) alternative futures for study. Each is briefly described below in terms of needs profiles. A diagram of the profile of the U.S.A. today is provided first as a basis for comparison.

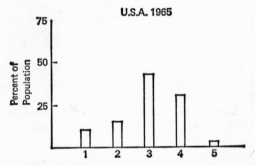

U.S.A. 1965

1. Survival orientation
2. Security orientation
3. Belongingness orientation
4. Esteem orientation
5. Growth orientation

Momentum: U.S.A. 1990

The first alternative is what we call the "Momentum" society. It depicts the society we expect will evolve by 1990 if present trends continue. It was useful to construct this society for several reasons:

1. It provides a preview of what [many think] is most likely to happen. The safest forecasting assumption—other things being equal—is that what is happening today will continue to happen tomorrow. . . .
2. Study of the negative and positive aspects of the Momentum society might prove highly practical in identifying danger areas for immediate and intermediate time periods.
3. Study of the Momentum society might show that we need not concern ourselves with designing new futures—that what's coming will be just what's wanted.

As compared with the U.S.A. today, the Momentum society is generally displaced upwards in need levels. The peak need level shifts from belongingness to esteem; people at the survival level almost disappear and those at the growth level jump from 2% to perhaps 12% of the population. There is relatively little change in the numbers operating modally at the safety level.

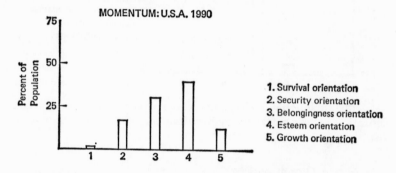

MOMENTUM: U.S.A. 1990

1. Survival orientation
2. Security orientation
3. Belongingness orientation
4. Esteem orientation
5. Growth orientation

A measure of the total amount of change implied in achieving the Momentum society starting from today's base can be obtained by summing the differences in the column heights between the two need profiles. By this measure the Momentum society has a change index from today of 40.

Mature Belongingness Society

A second societal configuration is what we call a mature Belongingness (or Belonging) society. We hypothesized that the nation could elect to mount a gigantic educational effort to move most of its citizens now "hung up" at survival and safety levels to [a more collective mode] of life. If successful, these efforts might reduce the fraction of the population operating at levels 1 and 2 from 25% to perhaps 7%. A second change is an assumed drop in the esteem-oriented population from 30% to 20%. This drop might come to pass for two principal reasons. First, the societal effort required to move over 70% of the survival- and security-oriented people to the belongingness level is likely to be so massive as to drain away resources currently flowing to the esteem level. Secondly, the Belonging society attempts by its nature to impose a monolithic homogeneity on its citizens. One result of this would be to "drag down" to the belongingness level people who are insecurely ensconced at the esteem level. It is considered that growth-oriented people could withstand this external social pressure. For this reason, no change is foreseen in the ranks of level 5.

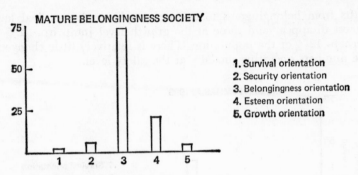

MATURE BELONGINGNESS SOCIETY

1. Survival orientation
2. Security orientation
3. Belongingness orientation
4. Esteem orientation
5. Growth orientation

The Belonging society involves a change from today's configuration of 68—markedly higher than the Momentum change index of 40. . . .

Mature Growth Society

The final social structure selected for analysis is called mature Growth society. The supposition here is that Americans very radically reoriented their [values] to produce growth-oriented people. It is further supposed that this transition is successfully accomplished, resulting, in the course of 25 years, in the needs distribution portrayed in the chart. The obvious feature is the heavy accent on level 5. It is imagined that some 60% of the population would operate at the growth mode, 25% at the esteem level, and the remaining 15% spread across the first three levels.

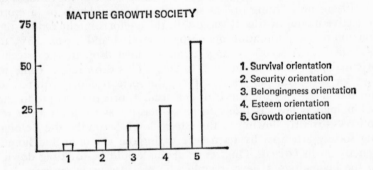

MATURE GROWTH SOCIETY

1. Survival orientation
2. Security orientation
3. Belongingness orientation
4. Esteem orientation
5. Growth orientation

The change index for this alternative future is 116— . . . almost triple the index of the . . . Momentum configuration. As a matter of practicality it almost certainly would be impossible to create a Growth society within a quarter century, starting from today's base. One problem is the paucity of off-the-shelf, proven knowledge of how to produce self-actualizing people. Even if we had the knowledge and know-how, we could hardly hope to find sufficient instructors to alter the need dominions, often by several levels, of essentially all of the population (well over 90%). Reliance would have to be placed on wholly new mass and/or self-induced and/or chemical or physical means of producing attitude change. Assuming success in this venture, side effects might well disrupt the nation's economic and institutional machinery to a degree that would be more conducive to revolution than to the building of a Growth society. For these and other reasons the Growth configuration is viewed as much more difficult to attain than the Momentum [or] Belongingness . . . societies. It nevertheless has been included in the same time frame (1990) as the others because such parallel treatment should provide some insight into whether the Growth society is an appropriate very long-term goal to pursue. . . .

SOME POSSIBLE VALUES AND GOALS OF FUTURE SOCIETIES

On the basis of the psychological orientations associated with each need level, it is possible to imagine how alternative future societies might conduct themselves. Our approach was to examine a variety of parameters that define a society and ask ourselves how each of the societies might differ from the U.S.A. of today. At this stage no attempt was made to quantify differences; for the purposes of this pilot exploration, indications of the direction of differences were considered sufficient. (In the charts that follow, upward arrows indicate greater emphasis relative to today, downward arrows indicate decreased emphasis, dashes suggest no change. The number of arrows is a rough indication of the presumed magnitude of the change, a single arrow denoting some, but not dramatic, change.)

Economic Orientations

In view of the varying values, attitudes, and interests of the modal groups of the five societies, rather large differences in growth rates of GNP should result. . . . A Belonging society, being less achievement-oriented than today's society, would probably place less stress on economic bigness, efficiency, and growth and greater stress on the family. The consequence probably would be a lowered growth rate in GNP, lower labor participation rates, faster population growth, and a marked decline in the trend for income per capita. We think that the Growth society would have about the same overall growth rate as the Momentum society. . . . But the route to economic expansion would be very different. We would expect a Growth society to be highly efficient, utilizing every technology to improve output per man-hour, so that all could be well cared for with fewer working much shorter hours. We believe—but the guess is hazardous—that a Growth society would not have a rapid population expansion, preferring quality to quantity and depth to breadth.

ECONOMIC PARAMETERS

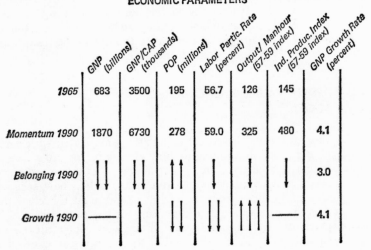

Institutional Orientations

The chart shows our judgments as to the relative emphasis we would expect in eight major institutional domains and five occupational realms. It would be possible to explain the reasoning behind each judgment. Hopefully, however, the reader by now has a feel for the hallmark qualities of each of the societies and will intuitively agree . . . with most of our judgments.

It should be pointed out that the ways in which the various societies would view institutions could be radically different, irrespective of the degree of emphasis relative to today's society. . . .

INSTITUTIONAL PARAMETERS

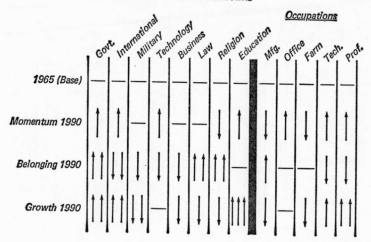

Religion provides a good example. We would expect a Belonging society to stress religion as an institution. Emphasis should fall on the formalized, tradition-dispensing, togetherness aspects of religion. . . . In our view, the Momentum . . . societ[y] might well drift away from institutionalized religion simply because [it] would find [its] kind of success more easily or more fully expressed in other endeavors—business, technology, [international] affairs, and the like. A downward arrow also appears in the religion column of the Growth society. What we think would happen is this: the "church visible" (in Santayana's wonderful phrase) would yield to a personal, interior type of religion. The society might well be more religious, but religion as an institution would nonetheless abate.

Other Dimensions

A variety of other sets of parameters were examined. Results are shown in the following series of charts. It would be possible to enlarge upon each in considerable detail, and discuss possible shades of quality for every indicated shift in societal direction. Even without such interpretation and expansion, however, the diagrams hopefully suggest our view of the broad sweep of the [three] societies under examination.

SOCIAL PARAMETERS

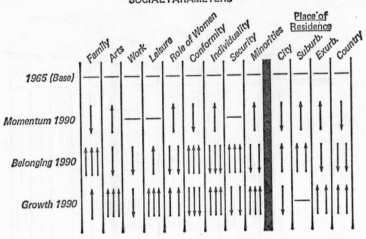

CONSUMPTION PARAMETERS

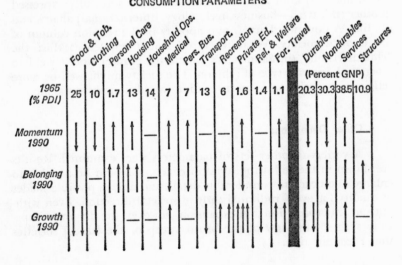

FEDERAL GOVERNMENT PARAMETERS

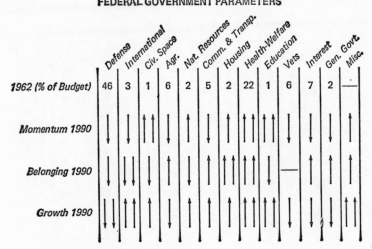

Way-of-Life Alternatives

Style-of-life constitutes a dimension of society that is hardly touched upon in the kind of analyses previously outlined. Quite clearly, it would be possible to have . . . a . . . society expressed in several different way-of-life modes, thus generating another sheaf of alternative futures. . . .

the issues
of tomorrow's work

If current trends continue, it is tempting to envision the possibility, by the late twentieth century, of settling back into lives of almost complete leisure and affluence. Unfortunately, the situation is not so simple. Economic projections forecast an increase in worldwide per capita wealth, but abundance societies are surrounded by a world of poverty. And global poverty is not the only challenge. Statistics on natural resources, signs of crowding and overpopulation, and a simple breath of city air warn us that we are on the brink of a major ecological crisis. Add to this the problems of maintaining our productive institutions, pursuing the emergent aspirations of an abundant life, and responding to new, unforeseen problems, and we are compelled to acknowledge that those living on islands of affluence cannot expect to avoid doing some type of work.

Recognition of growing global problems is unsettling when contrasted to emerging attitudes toward work in abundance societies. There are critical problems to be solved, problems that in many cases can only be solved by the material and knowledge resources of our most affluent areas. At the same time there are indications that the willingness to work, at least under current conditions, is declining. There are increasing cases of blue-collar workers sabotaging their assembly lines, corporate executives "dropping out" in midcareer, women demanding more than secretarial jobs, minorities refusing to do degrading tasks, and widespread youth alienation with the world of work.[1] This growing disenchantment suggests a potential crisis due to lagging work efforts in the face of mounting problems which may at best threaten the achievement of our fullest potentials and at worst jeopardize the survival of our species.

Whether we are primarily concerned with achieving the potentials of our time, or avoiding the dangers of societal collapse, it appears that a major concern of the coming decades will be to maintain and perhaps increase motivation to assume the responsibilities and pursue the opportunities of the future. In other words, to keep working. Yet, we know that the days are limited in which people will be truly productive under existing purposes and conditions of work.

The theories of Abraham Maslow (see second section) provide us with some indications of what we must do in order to maintain our productive motivation. The basic lesson of Maslow's "need hierarchy" theory is that there are priorities of needs and that once a need is satisfied, it is no longer a motivator. To switch this meaning around, we are only motivated by unfulfilled needs. Put in a concrete context, unlimited gold, particularly at the expense of other valued commodities, is, as the legendary King Midas found, of little or even negative value. Maslow also theorized that we are motivated by needs beyond material necessities such as the desires for love and belongingness, personal self-esteem, and for growth and exploration. Further, he shows us that we cannot truly pursue an "upper need" without having had fulfilled, and balanced the fulfillment of, "lower needs." From these observations we learn that high and perhaps better balanced motivation can be expected from our higher drives. Unfortunately, the realities of most contemporary work situations are still oriented toward material economic incentives. In short, if we are to move forward from our current isolated economic plateau, we must develop work conditions which truly deal with our higher and total needs.

We know today that work conditions providing integrated motivation focused upon individual priorities are possible. Manage-

[1] For further treatment of this widely based, growing crisis in work see Judson Gooding, *The Job Revolution* (New York: Walker and Company, 1973); Office of the Secretary, U.S. Department of Health, Education, and Welfare, *Work in America* (Washington, D.C.: December, 1972); "The Job Blahs: Who Wants to Work?" *Newsweek*, March 26, 1973, pp. 79; "The Great Escape: More Affluent Adults Quit Corporate World to Lead Simpler Lives," *Wall Street Journal*, February 19, 1971, p. 1; Dennis Derryck, "Young Blacks in the World," *New Generation*, January 11, 1971, pp. 22–26; Janet Sass, "B.A. Is No Job Guarantee," *Washington Post*, April 11, 1971, p. C2; Charles Phillips, "Grey Power," *America*, February 1969, p. 132.

ment science and technology provide us with studied models of work conditions and purposes which are more appropriate to our times. Indeed, many of these new approaches are being implemented at this time.

In the past sections we have dealt with the changing nature of work, the human thrust for departure, and the likely goals and values of future work activities. Now we are left with the concrete question of what the specific conditions of future work will be.

Section A

technology and automation: is work disappearing?

All discussions about the future of work seem to start out with the same question. Half humorously, someone is bound to ask, "Will there be work in the future?" The answer is both no and yes. No, in the sense that the activities and concerns we currently consider work are likely to disappear. Yes, in that we will undoubtedly find new goals and problems which will motivate entirely new forms of purpose-oriented or work activity.

The disappearance or de-emphasis of those activities currently considered work can be seen in our daily lives. The most graphic example comes from agriculture. Eighty years ago, raising food directly involved some 60 percent of our working population and was the major form of work. Today scarcely 5 percent of our workers are directly involved in primary food production, and the proportion is still dwindling. Statistics also show that the proportion of those involved in the manufacturing industries has leveled off and started to decline. The decline of agricultural and manufacturing work has allowed the evolution of a "service economy," in which the majority of our labor force is involved in producing such nontangibles as automobile repair, clothes cleaning, and law.

The primary cause for the disappearance of past forms of work is technological advance, specifically mechanization, automation, and cybernetics. The impact of such advance becomes evident when we confront R. Buckminster Fuller's observation that machines are essentially "stored energy and information." To put it another way, machines are extensions of human concern that store and channel energy in ways which human experience has learned are productive. The importance of automatic machinery becomes fundamental when combined with the multiple programming opportunities allowed by computers, to create what is called cybernation. In essence, cybernetic systems require fewer persons to control and operate more machines—one person assisted by the decision-making and electronic-activating resources of a computer may, for example, be able to operate and supervise an entire hydroelectric or oil refining plant. Machines in general, and cybernation in particular, afford humanity the potential to ultimately turn over to a machine system any routine or predictable task. The rapidity with which we surrender our existing work obligations to cybernetic systems is itself an issue subject to the variables of human priorities, investment resources, forthcoming technical innovations, and other factors. The essential point is that we are likely to continue to displace human work effort by machines and that this trend will probably accelerate. To hazard a crude prediction, within forty years or less, almost all the human activities now regarded as work will be assumed by technological devices of one form or another. In this sense, the work we know today *is* disappearing. It is unlikely, however, that work itself will disappear. But it will change fundamentally. Maslow's comments, in the preceding section, about "metamotivation" and the human capacity to find some suboptimization or discontent in even the most ideal of circumstances, suggest that we will find new frontiers of endeavor and goals for work.

The accelerating growth and diversification of technology is too complex to treat here or even in a volume many times larger. This section, therefore, presents selections chosen to convey the basic thrust and significance of technology in relation to work. First economic historian Robert Heilbroner seeks to put technological advancement into an evolutionary perspective and to point out that such advancement takes place when and where the need is most felt. He further shows that technology has fundamentally altered the conditions and goals of work. Then, management consultant Peter Drucker predicts the development and growing prominence of "the knowledge worker," who will be primarily concerned with the creation, communication, and application of society's knowledge. Work will not disappear, but the "knowledge worker" will become the "new proletariat," working under more autonomous, less-routinized conditions to create new goals and options for future human endeavor.

Chapter 4

work and technological priorities: a historical perspective

Robert Heilbroner

There is good reason why there is so much disagreement about automation. At least two of the reasons are obvious, and I will only state them in passing. One is the fact that we don't have enough figures, numbers, statistics. . . .

The second reason is equally apparent. We happen to be in a period in which the forces bearing on the labor market are unusually complex. We are, as you know, at a time when the labor bulge is coming down the pipe, so to speak, as the war babies come of age and take the bread from our mouths. At the same time, we are in a period of technological change. When you find an individual unemployed person, it is not always easy to know whether he is unemployed because the supply and demand situation is out of whack, or because he was bumped and not hired on account of some machine.

But there is a third reason why there is disagreement, and this is the one that I want to talk about. This is because there is a very curious lack of interest in the problem. There is a curious aversion to looking at the problem of technology and the market society.

I am struck by the fact that the two greatest economists of mature capitalism, Alfred Marshall and Lord Keynes, each wrote about capitalism and explicitly omitted technical change from their formulations. This is an astonishing fact when one considers that of all the phenomena characteristic of this system, the one that is by all odds, by general agreement, the most important is technical change. . . .

"Work and Technological Priorities: A Historical Perspective" (editor's title). From Robert Heilbroner, *Automation in the Perspective of Long-Term Technological Change*, Seminar on Manpower Policy and Program, U.S. Department of Labor (Washington, D.C., 1966), pp. 4–15.

INTERNAL EXODUS OF THE LABOR FORCE

First, let me call your attention to what I think is the fundamental setting of the employment problem—a setting that has to be explained and that also has to be taken into account in looking at today's and tomorrow's employment problem. This fundamental setting is what can best be described as an enormous internal exodus in the American economy, moving from some kinds of jobs into other kinds of jobs, but in a systematic, not in a haphazard way. Briefly, it is a streaming from the farm through the factory and into the offices. Let me give the magnitudes that this involves.

If we start back in the year 1800 and ask ourselves, "Where did people work?" the answer is that the great majority worked in agriculture.

Now, there was much less specialization of labor in those days than today, so that a person who was a farmer could very likely also do some manufacturing at home and supply himself with certain services. But nevertheless, there is no doubt that his main contribution to the economy was to raise crops. Roughly speaking, 70 to 80 percent of the people who lived in America in 1800 were essentially farmers. The other 20 or 30 percent were split between two other broad categories of occupations. Some of them—blacksmiths, tanners, printers—handled goods of various sorts. Some of them—legislators, merchants, clerks—provided services of various sorts. I don't think any figures show how the 20 or 30 percent that weren't essentially farmers were divided between services and goods, but however the division fell, in any event, the proportions in either category were clearly small. . . .

Now, finally, we bring the picture up to date and take you down to the present, where the general trend continues. Today, we have but 8 percent of the labor force on the farms, and that includes, as we all know, people who are just stuck there. It is effectively 5 or 6 percent who really raise food, the others are just disguised unemployed. About 40 percent, roughly the same percentage (it is really slightly more) is in the goods sector. And there is an enormous increase in the services. Over 50 percent of the Nation's working force push papers.

Now, this long secular swing out of agriculture through the factories and into the offices is a phenomenon of the most fundamental force, it seems to me; and it must be, in the first instance, explained, and, in the second instance, made relevant to technical change. That is what I would like to do.

When we ask why the exodus took place, what it was that pushed people off the farms and into the factories and then again through the factories and into the offices, the answer is very clearly an interaction of two economic forces, like the famous blades of the scissors in Marshall's description of supply and demand. In this case, however, the two forces are, instead of supply and demand, technology and demand. Behind the shift from agriculture, that is, behind the shift from the farm to the city and from the factory to the city to the office in the city, one of the propelling forces was clearly the introduction of machinery.

SEQUENCE OF TECHNOLOGICAL INTRODUCTION

There is, in the background of that force, an important characteristic which is not often noted. Machinery was not fed into the American economy, so to speak, at random, haphazardly, but in a certain grand sequence. The sequence was that the first area of occupations where technology lit and did its work was agriculture, and the second area where technology lit and did its work was the goods sector, and the third and last was the service sector. . . .

That grand sequence of inventions is not, I think, a mystical or fortuitous occurrence. In a market society we would expect the bulk of men's economic inquisitiveness to be directed to those activities that pay, and the activities that pay would tend to be, on the whole, the activities that occupy men's minds and that, in fact, bulk large in the spectrum of jobs. So that in an agriculturally centered society, we would expect to find inventiveness concerned with agricultural devices; in a society that gradually turns towards manufacturing, we would expect to find more invention, inventiveness, innovation, and, of course, more investment in those inventions directed towards the varieties of tasks having to do with handling goods. . . .

Now, the fact that technology came in this broad sequence—and I don't wish to press that point too hard—was not in itself the sole cause of the great exodus which is at the center of my discussion today. For the exodus would not have taken place had the effects of technology not been met with certain patterns of tastes or demands.

RACE BETWEEN TECHNOLOGY AND DEMAND

When we turn first to agriculture, which was the initial sector of the economy in which the effect of technology became noticeable, we note that between 1800 and 1850—I speak very generally—productivity more or less doubled. Had the demand for food doubled *pari passu*, there would have been no particular reason for farmers not to stay where they were. But, as we all know, the demand for food is very inelastic.[1] Here it became impossible for farmers to exercise the productivity that was theirs by virtue of their machinery and to make a living, or rather, for *all* of them to do so. As a result, they left the farm, or immigrants coming into the country did not go to the land, and stayed in the cities.

Between 1800 and 1900, the race between technology and demand on the farms was won by technology at the expense of the farmer, who moved to the city.

In the city, something rather different took place.

In 1869, which is for my purposes the midpoint of the century, half the motive power furnished in American industry was still provided by the water wheel—we were still at the level of paleotechnic culture. From 1869 to 1900, we saw the first burst of productivity-raising inventions applied on a large scale. So that we see in those years a very considerable growth in the output of goods, as opposed to farm goods. But matching this increase in the growth of goods is a concurrent increase in the demand for those kinds of goods— that is to say, for goods that have been taken from the earth, fabricated, processed, packaged, and transported to the point of sale. So that we find, during this second period, that factory employment— and I use "factory" in a very broad sense to include construction employment and transportation employment—expanded very considerably.

Then we enter a curious period from, let's say, 1900 down to the present. This is a period in which extraordinary inventions made

[1 The term *inelastic* refers to goods and services which have a stable or limited demand regardless of price. For example, if we have all the margarine that we can use for several weeks in our refrigerator, it is unlikely that we will want or need another pound. In this case our demand for margarine is inelastic. In short, there are some goods and services which we only want so much of regardless of price. Conversely, a good or service has elastic demand when a reduction in its price causes us to buy more of it. For further discussion see Paul Samuelson, *Economics,* 8th ed. (New York: McGraw-Hill Book Company, 1970), p. 357—Ed.]

their presence felt in the world of manufacturing of goods—not only inventions having to do with lowering costs and with increasing productivity, but inventions having to do with the creation of new kinds of goods, the so-called demand-creating inventions. The years from 1900 to the present were the years that witnessed the birth of such products as the automobile and the consumer durables, the new fabrics and plastics, airplanes, the modern technology of war, an enormous array in all. Virtually everything we think of as "manufactured goods" was invented and first produced around this period. So that surely this was a time when the demand for goods was stimulated as much as was ever the case in American history. . . .

In other words, by 1900 we had moved into the factories as large a percentage of the labor force, give or take a few percentage points, as we would need for the next extraordinary half century of demand creation.

Now, where did the rest of the people go? The numbers on the farm, not only proportionately but absolutely, fell all the while after 1900 and, indeed, in recent years, more rapidly than ever. Yet there was this extraordinary stability, this static quality, in the goods-handling sector—not just in manufacturing proper, let me repeat, but in the whole manufacturing, construction, mining, utilities, and transportation complex.

Well, we all know where people went. They went into that enormously varied group of occupations we call service occupations.

Now, here, too, demand was eager and absorptive, elastic. The most cursory survey of consumer spending shows a long steady swing from the earliest statistics towards spending one's income on these kinds of enjoyments. They correspond, perhaps on a national scale, to the experience of the individual who, at the simplest level of his existence, is forced to spend his subsistence on food; who then turns to the secondary tier of goods, his house, his clothes, and so on; but, when he is partially satisfied with those requirements, turns to the expenditures on services that have always marked the luxury expenditure pattern of the rich. Through history, as we in America have moved towards affluence, we have enjoyed proportionately more services.

But the service occupations alone in the grand spectrum of occupations were spared the other blade of the scissors, that is to say, they were spared—anyway, *relatively* spared—the incursion of productivity-enhancing technology.

Now let me hasten to say that some extraordinary inventions went into the service area. Automobiles, of course, greatly increased the mobility of the Nation. The telephone, the typewriter, were enormous things. Nevertheless, when you look at all the people who service you, you find vast areas where productivity actually didn't rise and, for all I know, fell. Teaching, for instance. It is very difficult to say that the productivity of a teacher today is significantly greater than it was in 1900. I just got a haircut when I got to the airport. God knows productivity there is lower. A million people work in restaurants today: Waiters, cooks, etc. Their productivity has only marginally improved, if at all. Janitors, sales clerks, file clerks—of the 30 or 35 million people who perform all these kinds of occupations, there are very large numbers whose productivity has scarcely been affected at all.

Now, that is, I think, an incontrovertible nutshell sketch of what has happened over the past 150 years. To recapitulate briefly, there has been an introduction of machinery of extraordinary productivity-enhancing effect on the farm and in the secondary echelon of occupations, and a much lesser degree of introduction of machinery into the tertiary sector; and there has been, matching that blade of the scissors, a certain pattern of demand-responsiveness. So far as food has been concerned, demand has been very inelastic; so far as manufactures have been concerned, elastic enough to provide a kind of stable layer of employment; and so far as services have been concerned, considerably elastic.

TECHNOLOGY ENTERING SERVICE SECTOR

Into that, I believe, incontrovertible description of what has taken place, I now inject a suggestion which is highly controvertible, but which, if true, may go a long way to explaining the furor that surrounds the word "automation" and to providing a kind of perspective for the problems that I think we face.

My suggestion is very simply that we have now reached the stage where technology is belatedly making its entrance into the third sector.

Now, in terms of the earlier hypothesis that I hold with Professor Schmookler, that invention follows the lure of profit, one would expect the service occupations which now bulk so large in the spectrum, occupy so much of our attention, and drain so much of our costs, to be interesting to work with from a profit-potential point of view.

In addition, we have reached a level of technological sophistication which simply makes it possible to do things that begin to duplicate the somewhat more "intellectual" kinds of tasks performed in the third sector, as contrasted, perhaps, with the second and first. But I can't verify, I can only suggest, this invasion by machinery into the third sector. I am forced back to that worst of all economic proofs—my impressions. Impressionism is good enough for art, it is not good enough for economics. But impressions are nevertheless powerful.

When I go to the banks and see their extraordinary check-reading equipment, I know what an impact this kind of machinery can have on office employment. But it is not just electronic check-readers that makes me think technology is taking a new turn. Another impression—and I am very well aware that impressions don't prove a point—derives from the bowling alley where my two boys go on Sunday. Last year it had in back of it a little hamburger and milkshake dispensary which was manned by a warmblooded human being. This year he is no longer there; and in his place is a machine that dispenses hamburgers and milkshakes. Vending machinery is very important.

In the stores, the drift towards self-help—which doesn't require any technology at all—is nevertheless an innovation, an organizational innovation, which has the same impact as the most highly sophisticated electronic computer. In the offices, the new machinery is everywhere visible, doing "clerk's" or "steno's" work.

Now, what I am suggesting is that potentially the most important development going on in the field of technology and its interaction with economics is the introduction of machines into these hitherto sacrosanct or relatively sacrosanct areas of employment.

I am not certain that modern automation machinery is more labor-displacing in the factory than old-fashioned machinery. I see no reason *a priori,* and I don't know of any facts *a posteriori,* that would prove to me that $100 worth of automation or $100 worth of electronics hooked up on a lathe will displace any more people than $100 worth of forklift trucks or overhead conveyers. . . .

NO EXPANSIVE MARKET LEFT

If it is true that there is this underlying trend of technology into the service occupations, it bears a very important implication for the future. It means that the last sector of the market economy has been, so to speak, preempted by machinery and that there is now no expansive market sector left.

Prior to this time, there was always an expansive market sector; going back to the 19th century the goods-handling sector was expansive, and coming into the 20th century the services have been expansive. As people got displaced elsewhere, the very forces of supply and demand in the market place brought them largely into private jobs in the service sector. If it is now true that machines are going to displace more and more people who do service jobs, the question is: Where will they go? . . .

Chapter 5

evolution of the knowledge worker

Peter Drucker

The "knowledge industries," [1] which produce and distribute ideas and information rather than goods and services, accounted in 1955 for one-quarter of the U.S. gross national product. This was already three times the proportion of the national product that the country had spent on the "knowledge sector" in 1900. Yet by 1965, ten years later, the knowledge sector was taking one-third of a much bigger national product. In the late 1970's it will account for one-half of the total national product. Every other dollar earned and spent in the American economy will be earned by producing and distributing ideas and information, and will be spent on procuring ideas and information.

From an economy of goods, which America was as recently as World War II, we have changed into a knowledge economy.

The figures are impressive enough. Ninety per cent of all scientists and technologists who ever lived are alive and at work today. In the first five hundred years since Gutenberg, from 1450 to 1950, some thirty million printed books were published in the world. In the last twenty-five years alone an equal number has appeared. Thirty years ago, on the eve of World War II, semiskilled machine operators, the men on the assembly line, were the center of the American work force. Today the center is the knowledge worker, the man or woman who applies to productive work ideas, concepts,

[1] The term was coined by the Princeton economist Fritz Machlup in his book *Production and Distribution of Knowledge in the United States* (Princeton: Princeton University Press, 1962).

and information rather than manual skill or brawn. Our largest single occupation is teaching, that is, the systematic supply of knowledge and systematic training in applying it.

In 1900 the largest single group, indeed still the majority, of the American people, were rural and made a living on the farm. By 1940, the largest single group, by far, were industrial workers, especially semiskilled (in fact, essentially unskilled) machine operators. By 1960, the largest single group were what the census called "professional, managerial, and technical people," that is, knowledge workers. By 1975, or, at the latest by 1980, this group will embrace the majority of Americans at work in the civilian labor force. . . .

But the statistics, impressive though they are, do not reveal the important thing. What matters is that knowledge has become the central "factor of production" in an advanced, developed economy.

Economists still tend to classify the "knowledge industries" as "services." As such, they contrast them with the "primary" industries—agriculture, mining, forestry, and fishing, which make available to man the products of nature—and with the "secondary" industries—that is, manufacturing. But knowledge has actually become the "primary" industry, the industry that supplies to the economy the essential and central resource of production. The economic history of the last hundred years in the advanced and developed countries could be called "from agriculture to knowledge." Where the farmer was the backbone of any economy a century or two ago—not only in numbers of people employed, but in importance and value of what he produced—knowledge is now the main cost, the main investment, and the main product of the advanced economy and the livelihood of the largest group in the population. . . .

"Knowledge" rather than "science" has become the foundation of the modern economy. This has already been mentioned in Part One, but it needs to be said again. To be sure, science and scientists have suddenly moved into the center of the political, military, and economic stage. But so have practically all the other knowledge people. It is not just the chemists, the physicists, and the engineers who get fat on consulting assignments—to the point where they may have a larger income from consulting outside the university than from teaching and research inside. Geographers, geologists, and mathematicians, economists and linguists, psychologists, anthropologists, and marketing men are all busy consulting with governments, with industry, with the foreign aid program, and so on. Few areas of learning are not in demand by the organizations of our pluralist society. There is, I admit, little call for the consulting services of the classics faculty.[2] But there is more demand for the theologians than most people realize. Altogether it is the exceptional area of knowledge which is not today being brought into play in business and industry, in government and the military, in the hospital and in international relations.

This demand, in turn, reflects the basic fact that knowledge has become productive. The systematic and purposeful acquisition of information and its systematic application, rather than "science" or "technology," are emerging as the new foundation for work, productivity, and effort throughout the world. . . .

The demand ahead for knowledge workers seems insatiable. In addition to a million computer programmers, the information industry in the United States will need in the next fifteen years another half-million systems engineers, systems designers, and information specialists. We will need, perhaps, two million health care professionals—nurses, dietitians, medical and X-ray technologists, social and psychiatric case workers, physical therapists, and so on. These people are both highly trained, well beyond secondary school, and highly skilled. They are fully the equivalent of the skilled machinist or the skilled carpenter with his years of apprenticeship. But their skill is founded on knowledge. . . .

These examples bring out some fundamentals of the knowledge economy.

1. Knowledge work does not lead to a "disappearance of work." Eminent doctors tell us today that work is on its deathbed in the rich, industrially advanced countries, such as the United States, Western Europe, or Japan. The trends are actually running in the opposite direction. The typical "worker" of the advanced economy, the knowledge worker, is working more and more, and there is demand for more and more knowledge workers. The manual worker, the typical worker of yesterday, may have more leisure. He may go home at five in the evening, but the knowledge worker everywhere works increasingly longer hours. The young engineer, the accountant, the medical technologist, and the teacher take work home with them when they leave the office. Knowledge work, like all productive work, creates its own demand. And the demand is apparently unlimited.

2. Knowledge does not eliminate skill. On the contrary, knowledge is fast becoming the foundation for skill. We are using knowledge more and more to enable people to acquire skills of a very

---

[2] Though Bible scholars are highly prized by both Israeli and Arab armies as consultants on topography, hidden water resources, and so forth.

advanced kind fast and successfully. Knowledge without skill is un-productive. Only when knowledge is used as a foundation for skill does it become productive. Then it enables us to acquire in less time and with less effort what it took years of apprenticeship to learn. It enables us to acquire new skills, i.e., computer programming, which could never be acquired through apprenticeship alone. Knowledge, that is, the systematic organization of information and concepts, is therefore making apprenticeship obsolete. Knowledge substitutes systematic learning for exposure to experience. . . .

The man or woman who has once acquired skill on a knowl-edge foundation has learned to learn. He can acquire rapidly new and different skills. Unlike apprenticeship, which prepares for one specific craft and teaches the use of one specific set of tools for one specific purpose, a knowledge foundation enables people to un-learn and to relearn. It enables them, in other words, to become "tech-nologists" who can put knowledge, skills, and tools to work, rather than "craftsmen" who know how to do one specific task one specific way. . . .

3. But while knowledge eliminates neither work nor skill, its introduction does constitute a real revolution both in the produc-tivity of work and in the life of the worker.

Perhaps its greatest impact lies in changing society from one of predetermined occupations into one of choices for the individual. It is now possible to make one's living, and a good living at that, do-ing almost anything one wants to do and plying almost any knowl-edge. This is something new under the sun.

Most of mankind through the ages has had no choice at all. Son followed father. The Indian caste system only gave religious sanction to what was the norm for most people. Of course, there was always some mobility, upward and downward; even the caste system in India could not entirely prevent this. But these were the excep-tions, the few lucky ones, the occasional highly gifted one, the victim of war and catastrophes, or the totally improvident who gambled or gave away whatever he inherited. And in a world in which most people eked out a bare subsistence on the land, being a peasant was for most of mankind the one and only occupation.

A century ago even the educated man could only make a living through knowledge in a few narrowly circumscribed "professions": clergyman, physician, lawyer, and teacher, plus—the one newcomer —civil servant. Engineers came in at the end of the last century. . . .

At the same time, access to education is becoming the birth-right of people in advanced societies—and its absence the badge of "class domination." It is the absence of access to education which is now meant when people in the developing countries speak of "colonial oppression" or "neocolonialism." Education a hundred years ago was still a privilege. Around 1850, it first became an opportunity which the educational systems in the developed countries increasingly made available to the gifted and ambitious among the poor and "underprivileged." Within the last twenty or thirty years, access to education has become a right. Nowhere is it yet guaranteed in the Constitution. But it is clearly as important today as any of the rights written into the Bill of Rights. Indeed, when the U.S. Supreme Court outlawed "separate but equal" education for the American Negro and ordered the integration of our schools in 1954, it clearly assumed that the right of access to education was as solemnly embedded in the American Constitution as any of the rights actually guaranteed therein.

4. Knowledge opportunities exist primarily in large organizations. Although the shift to knowledge work has made possible large modern organizations, it is the emergence of these organizations— business enterprise, government agency, large university, research laboratory, hospital—that in turn has created the job opportunities for the knowledge worker.

The knowledge opportunities of yesterday were largely for independent professionals working on their own. Today's knowledge opportunities are largely for people working within an organization as members of a team, or by themselves. . . .

The knowledge worker of today, in other words, is not the successor to the "free professional" of 1750 or 1900. He is the successor to the employee of yesterday, the manual worker, skilled or unskilled.

This is very substantial upgrading. But it also creates an unresolved conflict between the tradition of the knowledge worker and his position as an employee. Though the knowledge worker is not a "laborer," and certainly not a "proletarian," he is still an "employee." He is not a "subordinate" in the sense that he can be told what to do; he is paid, on the contrary, for applying his knowledge, exercising his judgment, and taking responsible leadership. Yet he has a "boss"—in fact, he needs to have a boss to be productive. And the boss is usually not a member of the same discipline but a "manager" whose special competence is to plan, organize, integrate, and measure the work of knowledge people regardless of their discipline or area of specialization. . . .

But the knowledge worker sees himself as just another "professional," no different from the lawyer, the teacher, the preacher, the doctor, the government servant of yesterday. He has the same education. He has more income. He has probably greater opportunities as well. He may realize that he depends on the organization for access to income and opportunity, and that without the investment the organization has made—and a high investment at that—there would be no job for him. But he also realizes, and rightly so, that the organization equally depends on him.

This hidden conflict between the knowledge worker's view of himself as a "professional" and the social reality in which he is the upgraded and well-paid successor to the skilled worker of yesterday, underlies the disenchantment of so many highly educated young people with the jobs available to them. It explains why they protest so loudly against the "stupidity" of business, of government, of the armed services, and of the universities. They expect to be "intellectuals." And they find that they are just "staff." Because this holds true for organizations altogether and not just for this or that organization, there is no place to flee. If they turn their backs on business and go to the university, they soon find out that this, too, is a "machine." If they turn from the university to government service, they find the same situation there. . . .

This clash between the expectations in respect to knowledge jobs and their reality will become sharper and clearer with every passing year. It will make the management of knowledge workers increasingly crucial to the performance and achievement of the knowledge society. We will have to learn to manage the knowledge worker both for productivity and for satisfaction, both for achievement and for status. We will have to learn to give the knowledge worker a job big enough to challenge him, and to permit performance as a "professional."

Section B

organizations: the changing work environment

In the modern world most of what is commonly called work is done within the context of one form or another of organization. This means that people have found that their efforts are more productive and rewarding when done cooperatively with others. And regardless of future changes concerning work, it is an odds-on prospect that work activities will still be done within some context of organizational cooperation. The deluge of advances in technology and in the understanding of human behavior suggests, however, that the nature of organizations will change.

In most cases the work of the past has been oriented toward the performance of routine and standardized tasks with the purpose of producing familiar or even traditional products. Whether we have been growing wheat, fastening doors to automobiles on the assembly line, or teaching twelfth grade algebra, our primary concern has been with the regular performance of known tasks to produce a predicted good or service. The result of this orientation was the evolution of a form of organization commonly called bureaucracy. According to sociologist Max Weber, bureaucracy is guided by three basic principles. First, participants are given specialized roles or functions which compliment and reinforce the roles of others in the organization. Second, overall organizational coordination and role assigning are assumed by a limited few through a hierarchy of command and authority. Third, the roles of participants are designed with the intention of permanence or stability.[1] To put it more concisely, bureaucracy puts people in set roles to perform generally predictable tasks on a routine or permanent basis. Essentially, in the absence of sophisticated cybernetic technology, bureaucracy has required people to use their bodies and minds as machines.

Today we are finding it humanly desirable and also more efficient to use machines rather than people to perform routine and predictable tasks. As a result the nature and purposes both of work

[1] See H. H. Girth and C. W. Mills (eds.), *From Max Weber: Essays in Sociology* (New York: Oxford University Press, 1958), Chap. 8.

and of organizations is changing. We are moving at progressively faster rates toward innovative forms of work or, to put it in another way, toward productive human concern with nonroutine or exploratory matters. Human cooperation will continue to be important, but it will require new forms of work organizations that are exceptionally flexible and which encourage efficient and total communication.

In this section I am including selections that illustrate the gradual assumption of permanent or routine functions by machines, the decline of organizational permanence and stability, and the pragmatic need for more communication and for multiple sources of change. In the first article, journalist Alvin Toffler provides a descriptive analysis of the growing trend toward temporary organizations which he calls ad-hocracies. Second, management scientist Warren Bennis cites the compelling need to replace old forms of authority with democratic participation in order to insure an organization's maximum receptivity and adjustability to changing needs and opportunities.

Chapter 6

ad-hocracy: the coming of temporary organizations

Alvin Toffler

One of the most persistent myths about the future envisions man as a helpless cog in some vast organizational machine. In this nightmarish projection, each man is frozen into a narrow, unchanging niche in a rabbit-warren bureaucracy. The walls of this niche squeeze the individuality out of him, smash his personality, and compel him, in effect, to conform or die. Since organizations appear to be growing larger and more powerful all the time, the future, according to this view, threatens to turn us all into that most contemptible of creatures, spineless and faceless, the organization man. . . .

What makes the entire subject so emotional is the fact that organization is an inescapable part of all our lives. Like his links with things, places and people, man's organizational relationships are basic situational components. Just as every act in a man's life occurs in some definite geographical place, so does it also occur in an organizational place, a particular location in the invisible geography of human organization.

Thus, if the orthodox social critics are correct in predicting a regimented, super-bureaucratized future, we should already be mounting the barricades, punching random holes in our IBM cards, taking every opportunity to wreck the machinery of organization. If, however, we set our conceptual clichés aside and turn instead to the facts, we discover that bureaucracy, the very system that is supposed to crush us all under its weight, is itself groaning with change.

The kinds of organizations these critics project unthinkingly into the future are precisely those least likely to dominate tomorrow. For we are witnessing not the triumph, but the breakdown of bureaucracy. We are, in fact, witnessing the arrival of a new organizational system that will increasingly challenge, and ultimately supplant bureaucracy. This is the organization of the future. I call it "Ad-hocracy." . . .

[BUREAUCRACY] CLIQUES AND COFFEE BREAKS

Before we can grasp the meaning of this odd term, Ad-hocracy, we need to recognize that not all organizations are bureaucracies. There are alternative ways of organizing people. Bureaucracy, as Max Weber pointed out, did not become the dominant mode of human organization in the West until the arrival of industrialism.

This is not the place for a detailed description of all the characteristics of bureaucracy, but it is important for us to note three basic facts. First, in this particular system of organization, the individual has traditionally occupied a sharply defined slot in a division of labor. Second, he fit into a vertical hierarchy, a chain of command running from the boss down to the lowliest menial. Third, his organizational relationships, as Weber emphasized, tended toward permanence.

Each individual, therefore, filled a precisely positioned slot, a fixed position in a more or less fixed environment. He knew exactly where his department ended and the next began; the lines between organizations and their sub-structures were anchored firmly in place. In joining an organization, the individual accepted a set of fixed obligations in return for a specified set of rewards. . . .

In turn, just as organizations endure for longer or shorter periods, so, too, does an individual's relationship with any specific organizational structure. Thus man's tie to a particular department, division, political party, regiment, club, or other such unit has a beginning and an end in time. The same is true of his membership in informal organizations—cliques, factions, coffee-break groups and the like. His tie begins when he assumes the obligations of membership by joining or being conscripted into an organization. His tie ends when he quits or is discharged from it—or when the organization, itself, ceases to be.

This is what happens, of course, when an organization disbands formally. It happens when the members simply lose interest and stop coming around. But the organization can "cease to be" in another sense, too. An organization, after all, is nothing more than a collection of human objectives, expectations, and obligations. It is, in other words, a structure of roles filled by humans. And when a reorganization sharply alters this structure by redefining or redistributing these roles, we can say that the old organization has died and a new one has sprung up to take its place. This is true even if it retains the old name and has the same members as before. The rearrangement of roles creates a new structure exactly as the rearrangement of mobile walls in a building converts *it* into a new structure.

A relationship between a person and an organization, therefore, is broken either by his departure from it, or by its dissolution, or by its transformation through reorganization. When the latter —reorganization—happens, the individual, in effect, severs his links with the old, familiar, but now no longer extant structure, and assumes a relationship to the new one that supersedes it.

Today there is mounting evidence that the duration of man's organizational relationships is shrinking, that these relationships are turning over at a faster and faster rate. And we shall see that several powerful forces, including this seemingly simple fact, doom bureaucracy to destruction.

THE ORGANIZATIONAL UPHEAVAL

There was a time when a table of organization—sometimes familiarly known as a "T/O"—showed a neatly arrayed series of boxes, each indicating an officer and the organizational sub-units for which he was responsible. Every bureaucracy of any size, whether a corporation, a university or a government agency, had its own T/O, providing its managers with a detailed map of the organizational geography. Once drawn, such a map became a fixed part of the organization's rule book, remaining in use for years at a time. Today, organizational lines are changing so frequently that a three-month-old table is often regarded as an historic artifact, something like the Dead Sea Scrolls.

Organizations now change their internal shape with a frequency—and sometimes a rashness—that makes the head swim. Titles change from week to week. Jobs are transformed. Responsibilities shift. Vast organizational structures are taken apart, bolted together again in new forms, then rearranged again. Departments and divisions spring up overnight only to vanish in another, and yet another, reorganization.

In part, this frenzied reshuffling arises from the tide of mergers and "de-mergers" now sweeping through industry in the United

States and Western Europe. The late sixties saw a tremendous rolling wave of acquisitions, the growth of giant conglomerates and diversified corporate monsters. The seventies may witness an equally powerful wave of divestitures and, later, reacquisitions, as companies attempt to consolidate and digest their new subsidiaries, then trade off troublesome components. . . .

Internal reorganizations almost inevitably follow such corporate swaps, but they may arise for a variety of other reasons as well. Within a recent three-year period fully sixty-six of the 100 largest industrial companies in the United States publicly reported major organizational shake-ups. Actually, this was only the visible tip of the proverbial iceberg. Many more reorganizations occur than are ever reported. . . .

"My own observation as a consultant," says D. R. Daniel, an official of McKinsey & Company, a large management consulting firm, "is that one major restructuring every two years is probably a conservative estimate of the current rate of organizational change among the largest industrial corporations. . . .

If the once-fixed table of organization won't hold still in industry, much the same is increasingly true of the great government agencies as well. There is scarcely an important department or ministry in the governments of the technological nations that has not undergone successive organizational change in recent years. . . . [Indeed] internal redesign has become a byword in Washington. In 1965 when John Gardner became Secretary of Health, Education and Welfare, a top-to-bottom reorganization shook that department. Agencies, bureaus and offices were realigned at a rate that left veteran employees in a state of mental exhaustion. (During the height of this reshuffling, one official, who happens to be a friend of mine, used to leave a note behind for her husband each morning when she left for work. The note consisted of her telephone number for *that* day. So rapid were the changes that she could not keep a telephone number long enough for it to be listed in the departmental directory.) Mr. Gardner's successors continued tinkering with organization, and by 1969, Robert Finch, after eleven months in office, was pressing for yet another major overhaul, having concluded in the meantime that the department was virtually unmanageable in the form in which he found it.

In *Self-Renewal,* an influential little book written before he entered the government, Gardner asserted that: "The farsighted administrator . . . reorganizes to break down calcified organizational lines. He shifts personnel . . . He redefines jobs to break them out of rigid categories." Elsewhere Gardner referred to the "crises of organization" in government and suggested that, in both the public and private sectors, "Most organizations have a structure that was designed to solve problems that no longer exist." The "self-renewing" organization, he defined as one that constantly changes its structure in response to changing needs.

Gardner's message amounts to a call for permanent revolution in organizational life, and more and more sophisticated managers are recognizing that in a world of accelerating change reorganization is, and must be, an on-going process, rather than a traumatic once-in-a-lifetime affair. . . .

The result is that man's organizational relationships today tend to change at a faster pace than ever before. The average relationship is less permanent, more temporary, than ever before.

THE NEW AD-HOCRACY

The high rate of turnover is most dramatically symbolized by the rapid rise of what executives call "project" or "task-force" management. Here teams are assembled to solve specific short-term problems. Then, exactly like the mobile playgrounds, they are disassembled and their human components reassigned. Sometimes these teams are thrown together to serve only for a few days. Sometimes they are intended to last a few years. But unlike the functional departments or divisions of a traditional bureaucratic organization, which are presumed to be permanent, the project or task-force team is temporary by design.

When Lockheed Aircraft Corporation won a controversial contract to build fifty-eight giant C-5A military air transports, it created a whole new 11,000-man organization specifically for that purpose. To complete the multi-billion-dollar job, Lockheed had to coordinate the work not only of its own people, but of hundreds of subcontracting firms. In all, 6000 companies are involved in producing the more than 120,000 parts needed for each of these enormous airplanes. The Lockheed project organization created for this purpose has its own management and its own complex internal structure.

The first of the C-5A's rolled out of the shop exactly on schedule in March, 1969, twenty-nine months after award of the contract. The last of the fifty-eight transports was due to be delivered two years later. This meant that the entire imposing organization created for this job had a planned life span of five years. What we see here is nothing less than the creation of a disposable division—the organizational equivalent of paper dresses or throw-away tissues.

Project organization is widespread in the aerospace industries. When a leading manufacturer set out to win a certain large contract from the National Aeronautics and Space Agency, it assembled a team of approximately one hundred people borrowed from various functional divisions of the company. The project team worked for about a year and a half to gather data and analyze the job even before the government formally requested bids. When the time came to prepare a formal bid—a "proposal," as it is known in the industry—the "pre-proposal project team" was dissolved and its members sent back to their functional divisions. A new team was brought into being to write the actual proposal.

Proposal-writing teams often work together for a few weeks. Once the proposal is submitted, however, the proposal team is also disbanded. When the contract is won (if it is), new teams are successively established for development, and, ultimately, production of the goods required. . . .

"In just a few years," says *Business Week*, "the project manager has become commonplace." Indeed, project management has, itself, become recognized as a specialized executive art, and there is a small, but growing band of managers, both in the United States and Europe, who move from project to project, company to company, never settling down to run routine or long-term operations. Books on project and task-force management are beginning to appear. And the United States Air Force Systems Command at Dayton, Ohio, runs a school to train executives for project management. . . .

George Kozmetsky, co-founder of Teledyne, Incorporated, and now dean of the school of business at the University of Texas, distinguishes between "routine" and "non-routine" organizations. The latter grapple most frequently with one-of-a-kind problems. He cites statistics to show that the non-routine sector, in which he brackets government and many of the advanced technology companies, is growing so fast that it will employ 65 percent of the total United States work force by the year 2001. Organizations in this sector are precisely the ones that rely most heavily on transient teams and task forces.

Clearly, there is nothing new about the idea of assembling a group to work toward the solution of a specific problem, then dismantling it when the task is completed. What is new is the frequency with which organizations must resort to such temporary arrangements. The seemingly permanent structures of many large organizations, often *because* they resist change, are now heavily infiltrated with these transient cells.

On the surface, the rise of temporary organization may seem insignificant. Yet this mode of operation plays havoc with the traditional conception of organization as consisting of more or less permanent structures. Throw-away organizations, *ad hoc* teams or committees, do not necessarily replace permanent functional structures, but they change them beyond recognition, draining them of both people and power. Today while functional divisions continue to exist, more and more project teams, task forces and similar organizational structures spring up in their midst, then disappear. And people, instead of filling fixed slots in the functional organization, move back and forth at a high rate of speed. They often retain their functional "home base" but are detached repeatedly to serve as temporary team members. . . .

So long as a society is relatively stable and unchanging, the problems it presents to men tend to be routine and predictable. Organizations in such an environment can be relatively permanent. But when change is accelerated, more and more novel first-time problems arise, and traditional forms of organization prove inadequate to the new conditions. They can no longer cope. As long as this is so, says Dr. Donald A. Schon, president of the Organization for Social and Technical Innovation, we need to create "self-destroying organizations . . . lots of autonomous, semiattached units which can be spun off, destroyed, sold bye-bye, when the need for them has disappeared." . . .

As acceleration continues, organizational redesign becomes a continuing function. According to management consultant Bernard Muller-Thym, the new technology, combined with advanced management techniques, creates a totally new situation. "What is now within our grasp," he says, "is a kind of productive capability that is alive with intelligence, alive with information, so that at its maximum it is completely flexible; one could completely reorganize the plant from hour to hour if one wished to do so." And what is true of the plant is increasingly true of the organization as a whole.

In short, the organizational geography of super-industrial society can be expected to become increasingly kinetic, filled with turbulence and change. The more rapidly the environment changes, the shorter the life span of organization forms. In administrative structure, just as in architectural structure, we are moving from long-enduring to temporary forms, from permanence to transience. We are moving from bureaucracy to Ad-hocracy. . . .

THE COLLAPSE OF HIERARCHY

Something else is happening, too: a revolutionary shift in power relationships. Not only are large organizations forced both to change their internal structure and to create temporary units, but they are also finding it increasingly difficult to maintain their traditional chains-of-command. . . .

This process is noticeable in industry where, according to Professor William H. Read of the Graduate School of Business at McGill University, "irresistible pressures" are battering hierarchical arrangements. "The central, crucial and important business of organizations," he declares, "is increasingly shifting from up and down to 'sideways.'" What is involved in such a shift is a virtual revolution in organizational structure—and human relations. For people communicating "sideways"—i.e., to others at approximately the same level of organization—behave differently, operate under very different pressures, than those who must communicate up and down a hierarchy.

. . . typically bureaucratic arrangement is ideally suited to solving routine problems at a moderate pace. But when things speed up, or the problems cease to be routine, chaos often breaks loose. . . .

It will be a long time before the last bureaucratic hierarchy is obliterated. For bureaucracies are well suited to tasks that require masses of moderately educated men to perform routine operations, and, no doubt, some such operations will continue to be performed by men in the future. Yet it is precisely such tasks that the computer and automated equipment do far better than men. It is clear that in super-industrial society many such tasks will be performed by great self-regulating systems of machines, doing away with the need for bureaucratic organization. Far from fastening the grip of bureaucracy on civilization more tightly than before, automation leads to its overthrow.

As machines take over routine tasks and the accelerative thrust increases the amount of novelty in the environment, more and more of the energy of society (and its organizations) must turn toward the solution of non-routine problems. This requires a degree of imagination and creativity that bureaucracy, with its man-in-a-slot organization, its permanent structures, and its hierarchies, is not well equipped to provide. Thus it is not surprising to find that wherever organizations today are caught up in the stream of technological or social change, wherever research and development is important, wherever men must cope with first-time problems, the decline of bureaucratic forms is most pronounced. In these frontier organizations a new system of human relations is springing up. . . .

BEYOND BUREAUCRACY

If it was Max Weber who first defined bureaucracy and predicted its triumph, Warren Bennis may go down in sociological textbooks as the man who first convincingly predicted its demise and sketched the outlines of the organizations that are springing up to replace it. At precisely the moment when the outcry against bureaucracy was reaching its peak of shrillness on American campuses and elsewhere, Bennis, a social psychologist and professor of industrial management, predicted flatly that "in the next twenty-five to fifty years" we will all "participate in the end of bureaucracy." He urged us to begin looking "beyond bureaucracy."

Thus Bennis argues that "while various proponents of 'good human relations' have been fighting bureaucracy on humanistic grounds and for Christian values, bureaucracy seems most likely to founder on its inability to adapt to rapid change . . ."

"Bureaucracy," he says, "thrives in a highly competitive undifferentiated and stable environment, such as the climate of its youth, the Industrial Revolution. A pyramidal structure of authority, with power concentrated in the hands of a few . . . was, and is, an eminently suitable social arrangement for routinized tasks. However, the environment has changed in just those ways which make the mechanism most problematic. Stability has vanished." . . .

Weber was keen enough to notice this, and he pointed out that "The extraordinary increase in the speed by which public announcements, as well as economic and political facts are transmitted exerts a steady and sharp pressure in the direction of speeding up the tempo of administrative reaction . . ." He was mistaken, however, when he said "The optimum of such reaction time is normally attained only by a strictly bureaucratic organization." For it is now clear that the acceleration of change has reached so rapid a pace that even bureaucracy can no longer keep up. Information surges through society so rapidly, drastic changes in technology come so quickly that newer, even more instantly responsive forms of organization must characterize the future.

What, then, will be the characteristics of the organizations of super-industrial society? "The key word," says Bennis, "will be 'temporary'; there will be adaptive, rapidly changing *temporary systems*." Problems will be solved by task forces composed of "relative strangers who represent a set of diverse professional skills."

Executives and managers in this system will function as coordinators between the various transient work teams. They will be skilled in understanding the jargon of different groups of specialists, and they will communicate across groups, translating and interpreting the language of one into the language of another. People in this system will, according to Bennis, "be differentiated not vertically, according to rank and role, but flexibly and functionally, according to skill and professional training."

Because of the high rate of movement back and forth from one transient team to another, he continues, "There will . . . be a reduced commitment to work groups . . . While skills in human interaction will become more important, due to the growing needs for collaboration in complex tasks, there will be a concomitant reduction in group cohesiveness . . . People will have to learn to develop quick and intense relationships on the job, and learn to bear the loss of more enduring work relationships."

This then is a picture of the coming Ad-hocracy, the fast-moving, information-rich, kinetic organization of the future, filled with transient cells and extremely mobile individuals. From this sketch, moreover, it is possible to deduce some of the characteristics of the human beings who will populate these new organizations— and who, to some extent, are already to be found in the prototype organizations of today. What emerges is dramatically different from the stereotype of the organization man. For just as the acceleration of change and increased novelty in the environment demand a new form of organization, they demand, too, a new kind of man. . . .

Writing about young executives in American industry today, Walter Guzzardi, Jr., declares: "The agreements between modern man and modern organization are not like the laws of the Medes and the Persians. They were not made to stand forever . . . The man periodically examines his own attitude toward the organization, and gauges its attitude toward him. If he doesn't like what he sees, he tries to change it. If he can't change it, he moves." Says executive recruiter George Peck: "The number of top executives with their résumés in their desk drawer is amazing."

The old loyalty felt by the organization man appears to be going up in smoke. In its place we are watching the rise of professional loyalty. In all of the techno-societies there is a relentless increase in the number of professional, technical and other specialists.

In the United States between 1950 and 1969 alone, their number has more than doubled and this class continues to grow more rapidly than any other group in the work force. Instead of operating as individual, entrepreneurial free lancers, millions of engineers, scientists, psychologists, accountants and other professionals have entered the ranks of organization. What has happened as a result is a neat dialectical reversal. Veblen wrote about the industrialization of the professional. Today we are observing the professionalization of industry.

Thus John Gardner declares: "The loyalty of the professional man is to his profession and not to the organization that may house him at any given moment. Compare the chemist or electronics engineer in a local plant with the non-professional executives in the same plant. The men the chemist thinks of as his colleagues are not those who occupy neighboring offices, but his fellow professionals wherever they may be throughout the country, even throughout the world. Because of his fraternal ties with widely dispersed contemporaries, he himself is highly mobile. But even if he stays in one place his loyalty to the local organization is rarely of the same quality as that of the true organization man. He never quite believes in it.

"The rise of the professions means that modern large-scale organization has been heavily infiltrated by men who have an entirely different concept of what organization is about . . ." In effect, these men are "outsiders" working within the system.

At the same time, the term "profession" is itself taking on new meaning. Just as the vertical hierarchies of bureaucracy break down under the combined impact of new technology, new knowledge, and social change, so too, do the horizontal hierarchies that have until now divided human knowledge. The old boundaries between specialties are collapsing. Men increasingly find that the novel problems thrust at them can be solved only by reaching beyond narrow disciplines. . . .

In this situation, even professional loyalties turn into short-term commitments, and the work itself, the task to be done, the problem to be solved, begins to elicit the kind of commitment hitherto reserved for the organization. Professional specialists, according to Bennis, "seemingly derive their rewards from inward standards of excellence, from their professional societies, and from the intrinsic satisfaction of their task. In fact, they are committed to the task, not the job; to their standards, not their boss. And because they have degrees, they travel. They are not good 'company men';

they are uncommitted except to the challenging environments where they can 'play with problems.' "

These men of the future already man some of the Ad-hocracies that exist today. There is excitement and creativity in the computer industry, in educational technology, in the application of systems techniques to urban problems, in the new oceanography industry, in government agencies concerned with environmental health, and elsewhere. In each of these fields, more representative of the future than the past, there is a new venturesome spirit which stands in total contrast to the security-minded, orthodoxy and conformity associated with the organization man.

The new spirit in these transient organizations is closer to that of the entrepreneur than the organization man. The free-swinging entrepreneur who started up vast enterprises unafraid of defeat or adverse opinion, is a folk hero of industrialism, particularly in the United States. Pareto labeled the entrepreneurs "adventurous souls, hungry for novelty . . . not at all alarmed at change."

It is conventional wisdom to assert that the age of the entrepreneur is dead, and that in his place there now stand only organization men or bureaucrats. Yet what is happening today is a resurgence of entrepreneurialism within the heart of large organizations. The secret behind this reversal is the new transience and the death of economic insecurity for large masses of educated men. With the rise of affluence has come a new willingness to take risks. Men are willing to risk failure because they cannot believe they will ever starve. Thus says Charles Elwell, director of industrial relations for Hunt Foods: "Executives look at themselves as individual entrepreneurs who are selling their knowledge and skills." Indeed, as Max Ways has pointed out in *Fortune*: "The professional man in management has a powerful base of independence—perhaps a firmer base than the small businessman ever had in his property rights."

Thus we find the emergence of a new kind of organization man—a man who, despite his many affiliations, remains basically uncommitted to any organization. He is willing to employ his skills and creative energies to solve problems with equipment provided by the organization, and within temporary groups established by it. But he does so only so long as the problems interest *him*. He is committed to his own career, his own self-fulfillment.

Chapter 7

organizational democracy:
towards work by consent
of the employed

Warren Bennis and Philip Slater

Cynical observers have always been fond of pointing out that business leaders who extol the virtues of democracy on ceremonial occasions would be the last to think of applying them to their own organizations. To the extent that this is true, however, it reflects a state of mind that by no means is peculiar to businessmen, but that characterizes all Americans, if not perhaps all citizens of democracies.

This attitude, briefly, is that democracy is a nice way of life for nice people, despite its manifold inconveniences—a kind of expensive and inefficient luxury, like owning a large medieval castle. Feelings about it are for the most part affectionate, even respectful, but a little impatient. There are probably few men of affairs in America who have not at some time nourished in their hearts the blasphemous thought that life would go much more smoothly if democracy could be relegated to some kind of Sunday morning devotion.

The bluff practicality of the "nice-but-inefficient" stereotype masks a hidden idealism, however, for it implies that institutions can survive in a competitive environment through the sheer good-heartedness of those who maintain them. We would like to challenge this notion and suggest that even if all of those benign sentiments were eradicated today, we would awaken tomorrow to find democracy still firmly entrenched, buttressed by a set of economic, social, and political forces as practical as they are uncontrollable.

We will argue that democracy has been so widely embraced not because of some vague yearning for human rights but because *under certain conditions* it is a more "efficient" form of social organization. We do not regard it as accidental that those nations of the world that have endured longest under conditions of relative wealth and stability are democratic, while authoritarian regimes have, with few exceptions, either crumbled or maintained a precarious and backward existence. . . .

Our position is, in brief, that democracy (whether capitalistic or socialistic is not at issue here) is the only system that can successfully cope with the changing demands of contemporary civilization. We are not necessarily endorsing democracy as such; one might reasonably argue that industrial civilization is pernicious and should be abolished. We suggest merely that given a desire to survive in this civilization, democracy is the most effective means to achieve this end.

There are signs, in fact, that our business community is becoming aware of this law. Several of the newest and most rapidly blooming companies in the United States boast unusually democratic organizations. Even more surprising is the fact that some of the largest of the established corporations have been moving steadily, if accidentally, toward democratization. Frequently they began by feeling that administrative vitality and creativity were lacking in the older systems of organization. In increasing numbers, therefore, they enlisted the support of social scientists and of outside programs, the net effect of which has been to democratize their organization. Executives and even entire management staffs have been sent to participate in human relations and organizational laboratories to learn skills and attitudes that ten years ago would have been denounced as anarchic and revolutionary. At these meetings, status prerogatives and traditional concepts of authority are severely challenged.

Many social scientists have played an important role in this development toward humanizing and democratizing large-scale bureaucracies. The contemporary theories of McGregor, Likert, Argyris, and Blake have paved the way to a new social architecture. Research and training centers at the National Training Laboratories, Tabistock Institute, Massachusetts Institute of Technology, Harvard Business School, Boston University, University of California at Los Angeles, Case Institute of Technology, and others have pioneered in the application of social scientific knowledge to the improvement of organizational effectiveness. So far, the data are not all in; conclusive evidence is missing, but the forecast seems to hold genuine promise: it is possible to bring about greater organizational effectiveness through the utilization of valid social knowledge.

What we have in mind when we use the term "democracy" is not "permissiveness" or "laissez faire," but a system of values—a climate of beliefs governing behavior—which people are internally compelled to affirm by deeds as well as words. These values include:

1. Full and free *communication*, regardless of rank and power.
2. A reliance on *consensus*, rather than the more customary forms of coercion or compromise to manage conflict.
3. The idea that *influence* is based on technical competence and knowledge rather than on the vagaries of personal whims or prerogatives of power.
4. An atmosphere that permits and even encourages emotional expression as well as task-oriented acts.
5. A basically human bias, one that accepts the inevitability of conflict between the organization and the individual, but that is willing to cope with and mediate this conflict on rational grounds.

Changes along these dimensions are being promoted widely in American industry. Most important, for our analysis, is what we believe to be the reason for these changes: *democracy becomes a functional necessity whenever a social system is competing for survival under conditions of chronic change.*

The most familiar variety of such change to the inhabitants of the modern world is technological innovation. Since change has now become a permanent and accelerating factor in American life, adaptability to change becomes increasingly the most important single determinant of survival. The profit, the saving, the efficiency, the morale of the moment becomes secondary to keeping the door open for rapid readjustment to changing conditions.

Organization and communication research at the Massachusetts Institute of Technology reveals quite dramatically what type of organization is best suited for which kind of environment. Specifically: for simple tasks under static conditions, an autocratic, centralized structure, such as has characterized most industrial organizations in the past, is quicker, neater, and more efficient. But for adaptability to changing conditions, for rapid acceptance of a new idea, for "flexibility in dealing with novel problems, generally high morale and loyalty . . . the more egalitarian or decentralized type seems to work better." One of the reasons for this is that the centralized decision-maker is "apt to discard an idea on the grounds that he is too busy or the idea too impractical." [1] The failure of Nazi Germany to develop the atom bomb is a telling example of this phenomenon.

Our argument for democracy rests on an additional factor, one that is fairly complicated but profoundly important in shaping our ideas. First of all, it is interesting to note that modern industrial organization has been based roughly on the antiquated system of the military. Relics of the military system of thought can still be found in terminology such as "line and staff," "standard operating procedure," "table of organization," and so on. Other remnants can be seen in the emotional and mental assumptions regarding work and motivation held today by some managers and industrial consultants.

By and large these conceptions are changing, and even the military is moving away from the oversimplified and questionable assumptions on which its organization was originally based. The Israeli army, for example, is unsurpassed throughout the world for sheer military effectiveness. It is also one of the most slovenly, equalitarian, and democratic. . . .

This change has been coming about because of the palpable inadequacy of the military-bureaucratic model, particularly its response to rapid change; and also because the institution of science is now emerging as a more suitable model.[2] . . .

We believe that science is winning out because the challenges facing modern enterprises are, at base, knowledge-gathering, truth-requiring dilemmas. Managers are not scientists, nor do we expect them to be. But the processes of problem solving, conflict resolution, and recognition of dilemmas have great kinship with the academic pursuit of truth. The institution of science is the only institution based on and geared for change. It is built not only to adapt to change, but to overthrow and create change. So it is—and will be— with modern industrial enterprises.

And here we come to the point. In order for the spirit of inquiry, the foundation of science, to grow and flourish, a democratic environment is a necessity. Science encourages a political view that is egalitarian, pluralistic, liberal. It accentuates freedom of opinion and dissent. It is against all forms of totalitarianism, dogma, mechanization, and blind obedience. As a prominent social psy-

---

[1] Bennis, W. G., "Toward a Truly Scientific Management: The Concept of Organizational Health," *General Systems Yearbook*, 1962, page 273.

[2] It would be a mistake to ignore the fact that there are many tasks for which the military-bureaucratic model is best suited, but it is precisely those tasks which are most vulnerable to automation.

chologist has pointed out, "Men have asked for freedom, justice and respect precisely as science has spread among them." [3] In short, we believe that the only way in which organizations can ensure a scientific *attitude* is by providing conditions where it can flourish. Very simply, this means democratic social conditions.

In other words, democracy in industry is not an idealistic conception but a hard necessity in those areas in which change is everpresent and in which creative scientific enterprise must be nourished. For democracy is the only system of organization that is compatible with perpetual change.

It might be objected here that we have been living in an era of rapid technological change for a hundred years without any noticeable change in the nature of the average industrial firm. True there are now many restrictions on the power of the executive over his subordinates compared with those prevailing at the end of the nineteenth century. . . .

If democracy is an inevitable consequence of perpetual change, why then have we not seen more dramatic changes in the structure of industrial organizations? The answer is twofold.

First, the rate of technological change is rapidly accelerating. Take advance in scientific knowledge as one criterion: it doubles every ten years. Casamir calculated that if the *Physical Review* continued to grow as rapidly as it had between 1945 and 1960, it would weigh more than the earth during the next century.[4] . . .

We are now beginning an era when a man's knowledge and approach can become obsolete before he has even begun the career for which he was trained. The value of what one learns is always slipping away, like the value of money in runaway inflation. . . .

Under such conditions, the individual *is* of relatively little significance. No matter how imaginative, energetic, and brilliant he may be, time will soon catch up with him to the point where he can profitably be replaced by someone equally imaginative, energetic, and brilliant, but with a more up-to-date viewpoint and fewer obsolete preconceptions. . . .

The second reason is that the mere existence of a dysfunctional tendency, such as the relatively slow adaptability of authoritarian structures, does not automatically bring about its disappearance. This drawback must either first be recognized for what it is or become so severe as to destroy the structures in which it is embedded.

[3] Sanford, N., "Social Science and Social Reform," Presidential Address for SPSSI, Washington, D.C., August 28, 1958.

[4] J. R. Oppenheimer, "On Science and Culture," *Encounter*, October, 1962, page 5.

Both of these conditions are only now beginning to make themselves felt, primarily through the peculiar nature of modern technological competition. . . .

This issue is frequently misunderstood. People argue that Nazi Germany was an exception to our rule, since it was at once highly authoritarian and highly efficient. But the fact that the organization destroyed itself in foolish military adventures is excluded from the criterion of efficiency in this example, as if survival were a detail of no importance. This is a common fallacy in industry: a management which saves a hundred thousand dollars through cost-cutting measures and provokes, in the process, a million-dollar wildcat strike, is more likely to be called efficient than one which saves $900,000 by doing neither! . . .

The martinet general whose beautifully disciplined fighting machine is wiped out by guerrillas will probably still lay claim to efficiency, but we need not agree with his assumption that efficiency consists in doing an irrelevant thing well. By such a definition the March Hare was efficient when he used the "best butter" to repair the Mad Hatter's watch. The Greeks cautioned against calling a man happy before he had achieved a peaceful death; we would caution against calling any organization efficient until it has met at least one new and unexpected threat to its existence.

The passing of years has also given the *coup de grâce* to another force that retarded democratization—the "great man" who with brilliance and farsightedness could preside with dictatorial powers at the head of a growing organization and keep it at the vanguard of American business. In the past he was usually a man with a single idea, or a constellation of related ideas, which he developed brilliantly. This is no longer enough.

Today, just as he begins to reap the harvest of his imagination, he finds that someone else (even, perhaps, one of his stodgier competitors, aroused by desperation) has suddenly carried the innovation a step further, or has found an entirely new and superior approach to it, and he is suddenly outmoded. How easily can he abandon his idea, which contains all his hopes, his ambitions, his very heart? His aggressiveness now begins to turn in on his own organization, and the absolutism of his position begins to be a liability, a dead hand, an iron shackle upon the flexibility and growth of the company. But he cannot be removed. In the short run the firm would even be hurt by his loss, since its prestige derives to such an extent from his reputation. And by the time he has left, the organization will have receded into a secondary position within the industry. It may even decay further when his personal touch is lost.

The cult of personality still exists, of course, but it is rapidly fading. More and more large corporations (General Motors, for one) predicate their growth not on heroes but on solid management teams.

Taking the place of the great man, we are often told, is the "organization man." A good many tears have been shed over this transition by liberals and conservatives alike. . . .

. . . What is particularly confusing in terms of the present issue is a tendency to equate conformity with autocracy, to see the new industrial organization as one in which all individualism is lost except for a few villainous individualistic manipulators at the top.

But this, of course, is absurd in the long run. The trend toward the organization man is also a trend toward a looser and more flexible organization in which roles are to some extent interchangeable and no one is indispensable. To many people this trend is a monstrous nightmare, but one should at least not confuse it with the nightmares of the past. It may mean anonymity and homogeneity, but it does not and cannot mean authoritarianism. . . .

While the organization man idea has titillated the imagination of the American public, it has masked a far more fundamental change now taking place: the rise of the "professional man." Professional specialists, holding advanced degrees in such abstruse sciences as cryogenics or computer logic as well as the more mundane business disciplines, are entering all types of organizations at a higher rate than any other sector of the labor market.

And these men can hardly be called organization men. They seemingly derive their rewards from inward standards of excellence, from their professional societies, from the intrinsic satisfaction of their standards, and not from their bosses. Because they have degrees, they travel. They are not good company men; they are uncommitted except to the challenging environments where they can "play with problems." . . .

Yet it must also be remembered that all democratic systems are not entirely so—there are always limits to the degree of fluidity which can be borne. Thus, it is not a contradiction to the theory of democracy to find that a particular democratic society or organization may be more conservative than some autocratic one. Indeed, the most dramatic violent and drastic changes have always taken place under autocratic regimes, for such changes usually require prolonged self-denial, while democracy rarely lends itself to such voluntary asceticism. But these changes have been viewed as finite and temporary, aimed at a specific set of reforms, and moving toward a new state of nonchange. It is only when the society reaches a level of technological development in which survival is dependent on the institutionalization of perpetual change that democracy becomes necessary. . . .

It is this fact that reveals the basis for the association between democracy and change. The old, the learned, the powerful, the wealthy, those in authority—these are the ones who are committed. They have learned a pattern and have succeeded in it. But when change comes, it is often the *uncommitted* who can best realize it, take advantage of it.

Democracy is a superior technique for making the uncommitted more available. The price it exacts is the pain of uninvolvement, alienation, and skepticism. The benefits it gives are flexibility and the joy of confronting new dilemmas. . . .

Section C

work and leisure:
future free-time options

Advances in cybernation and other forms of technology promise to reduce human participation in most present-day areas of work and foster the evolution of new forms of work in nonroutine or exploratory areas. However, technology will not remove the human necessity or desire for work. It will, however, take over some fundamental tasks involved in providing food, shelter, and other essentials and will allow us more choices concerning the type and amount of work we do. In terms of our daily lives, we are likely to use these expanding options to increase our consumption of goods and services, to make work situations more pleasant, or to give us more time away from work.[1] In coming years the particular combinations of these possibilities may vary greatly. In one sense or another, this will likely mean that the future will bring some reduction in average working time.

The issues of work and leisure mushroom into an endless progression of questions and semantic squabbles. Indeed, the basic task of defining the difference between work and leisure has perplexed scholars and philosophers for ages.[2] Clearly, such issues are too numerous and detailed to be covered completely here. This section seeks only to focus on future options for more free time and present the probable means by which individuals will actualize their free-time preferences. Economists Juanita Kreps and Joseph Spengler treat the cost of increased free time in terms of foregone per capita income up to 1985. Their article provides an informative, concrete vision of the choices between more consumption and more leisure time. I then present a summary of the deadlock over the forty-hour week during the last two decades and the feasibility of breaking the impasse by developing flexible work scheduling.

[1] David Riesman, *Abundance for What?* (Garden City: Doubleday & Company, Inc., 1964), pp. 140–85.

[2] Sebastian de Grazia, *Of Time, Work, and Leisure* (Garden City: Doubleday & Company, Inc., 1962), pp. 1–157; and Josef Pieper, *Leisure as the Basis of Civilization* (New York: Pantheon Books, Inc., 1952), pp. 19–82.

Chapter 8

future options for
more free time

Juanita Kreps and Joseph Spengler

GROWTH AND DIMENSIONS OF LEISURE

Today's worker receives the equivalent of a four-month holiday, paid, each year. If he followed his grandfather's schedule of hours per week, he could work from October through May, then vacation till October. Or if he preferred, he could work April through November, and ski all winter.

He takes his nonworking time in different forms, but in total he enjoys about 1200 hours per year more free time than did the worker of 1890. Moreover, he enjoys more years in which he doesn't work at all; he enters the labor force much later in life, and has several more years in retirement than his grandfather. In total, this increase at the beginning and the end of work life has given him about nine additional nonworking years. Yet, lest the worker of today be labeled a loafer, it should be noted that since he lives longer, he works more hours in his lifetime than his predecessor; if born in 1960 he will probably log about 6800 more hours than the male born in 1900.

The Forms of Leisure

On the average, the employed person worked 40.7 hours a week in 1963; in 1890 the average was 61.9. Paid holidays have increased by at least four per year during this period, to about six at present, and paid vacations averaging one and one half weeks per year have added at least six days free time annually. Sick leave

"Future Options for More Free Time" (editor's title). From Juanita Kreps and Joseph Spengler, "The Leisure Component of Economic Growth," *Report of the National Commission on Technology, Automation, and Economic Progress,* Appendix Volume II, *The Employment Impact of Technological Change* (Washington, D.C.: Government Printing Office, 1966).

amounts to the equivalent of one week, giving the following increases in nonworking hours per year between 1890 and the present:

Source	Approximate hours
Reduction in workweek (21.2 per week)	1100
Increase in paid holidays (4 days)	32
Increase in paid vacations (6 days)	48
Increase in paid sick leave (1 week)	40
Total increase	1220

Thus, the shortened workweek has accounted for most of the century's rise in free time during work life. The addition of nine years of nonworking time raises the male's number of years outside the labor force by about 50 per cent. If, instead of spending this free time in gaining additional education and in retirement, a man worked on the average two thousand hours per year during these years, he would work during his lifetime an additional eighteen thousand hours, or 435 hours per year (with a work-life expectancy of 41.4 years). Thus the amount of nonworking time bunched at the beginning and end of work life has grown by about one third the amount added annually through workweek reductions, added vacations, etc.

Labor Force Size and Composition

During the same period, however, increasing numbers of women have taken jobs outside their homes; the proportion of the adult population in the labor force has therefore remained relatively stable. Despite the fact that the changing sex composition of the labor force would appear to be shifting from men to women, the effect of better household appliances, smaller families, and the sharing of household tasks is to apportion the increased leisure to both sexes.

Potential Growth in Leisure

The increase in nonworking time that has characterized the American economy during the twentieth century has in some degree reflected preferences for leisure as compared with income. In broad terms, the summary statement that about two thirds of the century's productivity gains have been taken in the form of goods and one third in free time suffices, although this statement alone obscures important issues such as the forms leisure has taken (and the extent to which these forms were in accord with workers' preferences), the distribution of nonworking time among the population, and the offsets against this freed time; e.g., longer commuting time to work. If, however, society has taken roughly a third of its increase in output potential in the form of leisure, the alternative statements that present leisure (as compared with that available in 1890) is "worth" approximately $314 billion, or that GNP which includes the value of leisure as well as the value of goods and services is about $941 billion (instead of $627 billion), provide crude estimates of the dollar value of our growth in leisure. If account is taken not only of the increase in material goods and services but also of the amount of leisure created, per capita growth in the economic value of output has not slowed down significantly.

Of more importance for present purposes, perhaps, is the question of the possible growth of leisure in the future. Long-range projections of the growth in nonworking time in total have not been made, perhaps because of the difficulties inherent in anticipating man's future elasticity of demand for goods in terms of effort. Despite great public interest in particular issues—shortened workweek, early retirement, etc.—which will determine the pattern into which leisure will fall, the potential magnitude of our leisure component has received little explicit attention.

The dimensions of future leisure can be indicated under varying assumptions as to growth in productivity and preferences as between goods and leisure. In Table 1 the basic assumptions are: Between 1963 and 1985 the growth rate will be 4.1 to 4.2 per cent per year, population will grow by 1.5 per cent annually, and unemployment will average 4.5 per cent. Assuming no change in working time, the GNP at projected rates of growth would approximate $1544.5 billion in 1985, about two and one third times its present level in 1960 dollars. Per capita GNP would rise from $3181 to $5802, or more than 80 per cent, despite the increased population size.

These increases in total and per capita GNP are possible, then, if working time of roughly forty hours per week for an average of forty-nine weeks per year is continued. At the other extreme, if one supposes that all growth, except that amount necessary to hold per capita GNP constant at $3181, is taken in leisure time, the possible increases in free time are indicated in the remaining columns. The workweek could fall to twenty-two hours by 1985; or it would be necessary to work only twenty-seven weeks of the year; or retirement age could be lowered to thirty-eight years. If the choice were made to divert the new leisure into retraining, almost half the labor force could be kept in training; if formal education were preferred, the amount of time available for this purpose might well exceed the normal capacity to absorb education.

It is, of course, not likely that the workweek will drop to twenty-two hours or that retirement age will decline to thirty-eight years. Nor is it probable that during the next two decades workers will continue on their present schedules, thereby taking all productivity gains in the form of a greater quantity of goods and services. If, instead, two thirds of the output growth accrues as goods and services and one third as leisure, GNP would rise to more than a trillion dollars by 1980, and to \$1.3 trillion by 1985. Per capita GNP would increase to more than \$4400 by 1980 and to approximately \$5000 in 1985. (See Figure 1.)

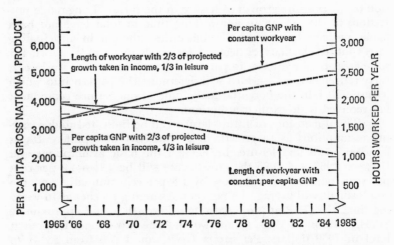

Figure 1. Alternative Uses of Economic Growth Per Capita Gross National Product and Hours Worked, 1965–85.
Source: GNP projections and employment data from National Planning Association, Report No. 65–1, March 1965. Labor force data for other computations taken from Manpower Report of the President, March 1965, p. 248, Table E-2.

The leisure which accounts for the remaining one third of the growth potential could be distributed in any one way or a combination of several ways; different priorities would be assigned by different persons. If it is conceded that present unemployment is due

Table 1 PROSPECTIVE GROWTH IN PRODUCTIVITY AND POSSIBLE USES OF RELEASED TIME

Year	Possible increases in real GNP (1960 dollars)			Alternative uses of potential nonworking time			Education and training	
	GNP (billions)	Per capita GNP	Total number of years	Retirement age	Length of workweek (hours)	Vacation time (weeks)	Labor force retrained[1] (per cent)	Years of extended education
1965	$627.3	$3181		65 or over	40	3	—	—
1966	655.6	3280	2,245,542	65	39	4	2.9	1.2
1967	685.6	3382	4,655,526	63	38	7	5.0	2.4
1968	707.1	3490	6,910,648	61	36	7	8.7	3.4
1969	745.3	3578	8,880,092	59	36	8	11.1	4.2
1970	779.3	3690	11,263,301	57	34	10	13.8	5.1
1975	973.4	4307	23,135,642	50	30	16	26.2	9.4
1980	1250.2	5059	35,586,729	44	25	21	37.2	13.8
1985	1544.5	5802	47,200,158	38	22	25	45.2	17.5

[1]Figures are in addition to the number of workers now trained in public and private programs.

Sources: GNP projections and employment data from National Planning Association, Report No. 65-1, March 1965. Labor force data for other computations taken from Manpower Report of the President, March 1965, p. 248, Table E-2.

in some significant degree to qualitative deficiencies in the labor force, however, the first priority might be assigned to job retraining. Hence, a policy decision could be made to retrain a minimum of 1 per cent of the labor force annually, taking the necessary time from that freed or released by the growth in productivity. A second order of preference might be an increase in vacation time, at least until an average of one additional week accrues to the worker. By 1968 these two goals—retraining 1 per cent of the labor force and increasing vacation time by one full week—could be attained. If after these achievements, some leisure gains are taken in the form of reductions in the workweek, working time per week could start by declining about one half hour in 1969, the decline increasing to two and one half hours by 1980. . . .

Alternative allocations of leisure in the period 1980–85 might be as follows: Given a $4413 per capita GNP in 1980, achieved with a 37.5-hour workweek, a forty-eight-week work year, and providing retraining for 1 per cent of the labor force, society could choose to retrain much more heavily (4.25 per cent of the labor force per year) or, alternatively, could add one and one half weeks per year in vacation. In 1985, when per capita GNP should reach about $5000, the choice could be between retraining almost 7 per cent of the labor force annually or taking an additional three weeks of vacation. Obviously, other choices could be made, involving a further reduction in the workweek, a lowering of retirement age, or an increased educational span for those entering the labor force.

The relevant considerations are at least threefold: One, the total amount of free time made available by the anticipated improvements in output per man hour is extremely great, even when allowance is made for quite rapid rises in real GNP or even in per capita real GNP. Two, the allocation of this leisure is in itself quite important, given the different degrees of utility man may associate with different forms of leisure. Three, the distribution of leisure, being quite unevenly spread over the entire population, requires further consideration. For although the unequal distribution of income among persons has received great attention, it might well be true that that portion of economic growth accruing to man in the form of leisure has in fact been apportioned much less evenly than income. Questions relating to the total volume, the forms, and the distribution of leisure are of some significance in estimating future potentials for growth in output, and particularly in determining the composition of that output.

Chapter 9

flexible work scheduling: beyond the forty-hour impasse

Fred Best

Conditions of life and work in contemporary abundance societies are often somewhat less than our hopes might lead us to expect. It takes little effort to conjure up a common, and perhaps frighteningly familiar, image of today's affluent worker. The stereotype of our times might be a white-collar industrial salesman in his mid-thirties who earns about $12,000 a year. With a little bit of effort we can imagine the style of his life. He spends between forty and fifty hours a week in frantic work activity and another five to ten hours commuting back and forth to work. During his time off the job he spends about eleven hours a day sleeping, eating, and dressing. Large parts of his remaining free time are spent planning his expenditures and buying goods and services. In the three hours or so left, he is likely to spend an hour and a half watching television, a large portion of which is composed of advertising telling him what to consume.[1] He may have a tennis racket and a set of golf clubs in his closet, and perhaps a sailboat at the ocean or lake. Yet he is lucky if he can get to his boat once a month for a day of frenzied sailing. He did not intend his life to be this way. Deep down he keeps dreaming of true leisure and some time in which he can let things settle and try to understand himself better. But for the most part, his life continues to be dominated by work and trips to the local shopping center. He is caught between his career and his daily routine, and there doesn't seem to be an opportunity to explore other

From the editor's forthcoming book. *The Post-Scarcity Juncture: Work Values and Quality of Life in Affluent Societies.* © 1973 by Fred Best. Used by permission of the author. This article appears for the first time in this volume.

[1] Basic time estimates were taken from John Robinson, "Social Change as Measured by Time Budgets," *Journal of Leisure Research,* Winter 1969, pp. 76–77 For an excellent discussion of the use of time in modern society, see Sebastian de Grazia, *Of Time, Work, and Leisure* (New York: Doubleday & Company, 1964).

possibilities. For too many people, this is the essence of postindustrial affluence.

But the wheels of our economy continue to turn, and the continuing growth of material well-being in advanced technological societies has become a modern legend. Between 1900 and 1970 per capita income in the United States jumped from $1,000 to over $4,000 in real dollars.[2] If current trends in productivity continue, we can expect an average U.S. family income of around $20,000 in the year 2000.[3] The prospect of this growing affluence introduces the possibility that large portions of our labor force will want to substitute other goals for potential material rewards—for instance, better working conditions and increased free time. All things considered, it is a safe bet that many of us will wish to forego some portion of our future income in exchange for more leisure time.

Throughout recent history, workers in affluent societies have constantly opted for more free time as incomes have risen. For example, in the United States the average work week dropped from sixty to forty hours between 1900 and 1940.[4] However, according to the Bureau of Labor Statistics, it has decreased by only three hours between 1940 and 1970.[5] For all practical purposes, despite massive strides in productivity, it has hardly become shorter during the last three decades. Still, workers have gained more free time in large chunks such as longer vacations, earlier retirement, more liberal sick leave, and later entry into the labor force.[6]

At the moment we appear to be caught in a stalemate concerning the forty-hour work week—an impasse which is the result of several factors. One major determinant has been the trend-setting effect of organized labor and the general failure of unions and management to negotiate reduced work weeks. Most union proposals for shorter weeks have been coupled with demands for continuance of the same overall pay; if workers earn $150 for a forty-hour week, the unions want them to earn the same for a thirty-five-hour week. To date, management has been unresponsive to such proposals, and the work week continues to linger at about forty hours.[7] Another force tending to stabilize the work week has been the tendency to

[2] Herman Kahn and Anthony Wiener, *The Year 2000* (New York: The Macmillan Company, 1967), p. 120.

[3] Ibid., p. 181.

[4] Sar A. Levitan, *Reducing Worktime as a Means to Combat Unemployment* (Kalamazoo, Mich.: The W. E. Upjohn Instiitute), September 1964, p. 4.

[5] Geoffrey Moore and Janice Hedges, "Trends in Labor and Leisure," *Monthly Labor Review*, February 1971, pp. 3–11.

[6] Ibid., p. 5.

[7] Levitan, *Reducing Worktime*, pp. 4–11.

increase free time in large chunks—through earlier retirement and the like. Such lumps of free time lend themselves well to extended travel, exploring new life-styles, and tackling major household projects. Doubtless we can expect large measures of future increases in free time to take this form. Most persons probably prefer it this way.

Today, however, many workers are seeking a larger variety of work-scheduling options than are currently available, and this growing diversity is making the formalization of a common work-scheduling format impossible. In San Francisco, for example, a young architect has assumed central design responsibilities for a low-cost housing research project. She sees her work as exciting, future-oriented, and personally rewarding. For her, working fifty or sixty hours a week is a usual and intrinsically motivated choice. But a few miles away at the General Motors plant in Fremont, there is a twenty-year-old assembly line worker with quite different views. A recent high school graduate who did not want to go to college and has to support himself, he took the job as a temporary necessity. He wanted to think a bit about his future and explore some options; however, now he finds that the forty-hour work week, commuting time, and personal maintenance matters leave him little free time for thinking things through or finding a better job. He is single and does not need full-time pay, yet he is forced into the standard forty-hour mold. In all sectors of life we find similar problems. There are housewives with master's degrees in social welfare who would like to work part time while their children are in school, fathers with family medical bills that require a period of extraordinary earning, artists who would like to work three months and take three months off, and college students who can't get jobs as sales clerks because stores "only hire full time." All these cases have a common theme: There is a need and desire for a greater variety of scheduling options in all areas of work.

In coming years we can expect a growing demand that we break out of the forty-hour work week impasse. It is improbable, however, that we will move toward a new hourly benchmark such as a standard thirty-hour week. Rather we can expect the development of attitudes and mechanisms that will allow flexible work scheduling and, therefore, better match the individual needs and preferences of workers to the goals and constraints of work organizations. But a word of caution: We must realize that alterations in working time entail more than a simple trade-off of income and consumption for more—or less—leisure. From the employer's perspective it will be necessary to develop some type of predictable interaction between participants which will promote maximum possible production in terms of both the individuals involved and organizational objectives. This necessity for worker predictability presents numerous complications; nonetheless, there is considerable room for vast liberalization of work-scheduling formats.

Today a variety of indications give promise of a movement toward flexible, individually oriented work scheduling. One is the evolution of the forty-hour–four-day week, in which people work ten hours a day for four days instead of eight hours a day for five. This version of a four-day week supports the theory that both employers and employees favor larger blocks of free time, even at the cost of more intense work periods. It also suggests that a coming issue of work scheduling may be the arrangement as well as the number of hours. Although the forty-hour–four-day week has become increasingly common, it is not likely to become the new standard. Rather its major significance probably lies in its precedent-breaking effect upon the traditional forty-hour–five-day week. Indeed, shortly after announcement of the first forty-hour–four-day week, a number of new and more varied versions began to appear. Riva Poor, who first chronicled the appearance of the four-day week, concludes her report with observations of burgeoning departures such as three-day weeks and four days on/four days off.[8]

Another indication of increasing work-scheduling flexibility is the introduction of "gliding work hours." Originally instituted by Lufthansa Airlines, this innovation allows employees who do not deal with the public during set business hours to arrive at work anytime between 8 A.M and 10 A.M. as long as they work a total of eight hours daily. In Europe this concept is being extended more and more to longer time contexts such as a week or a month. Reports on gliding work hours have been very positive from all perspectives. Employees appreciate the option of sleeping late on occasion and taking care of personal business during the work week. Employers find that organizational continuity has not been disrupted, employee morale has improved, and overtime problems are reduced.[9] Actually, the introduction of gliding work hours represents an extension of professional prerogatives. Traditionally, professionals are expected to assume personal responsibility for the adequate performance of certain duties within the context of a

---

[8] Riva Poor, *4 Days, 40 Hours* (Cambridge, Mass.: Bursk and Poor Publishing, 1970).

[9] Dennis Weintraub, "Starting the Work Day When You Want," *San Francisco Chronicle*, June 23, 1972, p. 23.

deadline rather than a timetable. Extending such scheduling dis-
cretions suggests there is a growing realization that people at all
levels exert greater effort and conscientiousness when entrusted with
freedom and responsibility.[10]

Another work-scheduling innovation which has made its appearance in the last few years is "group jobs." This means hiring a
group of persons—a family or perhaps a commune—to assume an
ongoing responsibility for, say, typing, answering telephones, deliv-
ering newspapers, or running a restaurant. From the employees'
viewpoint, it allows a great amount of individual variability as well
as a means of sharing both work and income with others. From
management's perspective, it will doubtless need more trial and development before being widely accepted. However, this concept
holds promise of reducing absenteeism in critical jobs and providing a readily available source of expanded manpower for unexpected
workloads and emergency projects. Incidences of group jobs are ad-
mittedly rare, but they are popping up in increasing numbers. The
group job is similar to gliding work hours in that it has been common at professional and executive levels in areas like consulting
firms and advertising teams; now the same idea is being extended
to many other forms of work.

The innovations described above seem to be harbingers of vast
expansions of flexibility in work scheduling. Indeed, once we free
our minds of the forty-hour habit and take a hard look at what the
real constraints are, our imaginations can virtually explode with
ideas for work scheduling. Some interesting work has been done in
this area by Philip Bosserman of the Center for Leisure in Tampa,
Florida. Bosserman foresees extending flexible scheduling from the
daily or weekly context to the monthly and yearly timespace, and
he envisions people working such combinations as six weeks on and
three weeks off or six months on and six months off.[11] To be sure,
such long-range scheduling plans may not be applicable to some
jobs. However, this idea could probably be applied to the vast majority of work conditions, with a gain of significant benefits by employers and employees alike. Specifically, jobs which are routine and

[10] It has been found that persons with highly flexible work hours exert
more time and effort on their jobs when they are dealing with an objective rather
than a time obligation. See Harold Wilensky, "The Uneven Distribution of
Leisure: The Impact of Economic Growth on 'Free-Time,'" *Social Problems*,
Summer 1961, p. 40.

[11] Philip Bosserman, *Youth and Leisure*, Background Paper for the Task
Force on Economy and Employment, White House Conference on Youth (Washington, D.C., 1971), p. 32. For other ideas on long-range scheduling, see Kahn
and Wiener, *The Year 2000*.

boring might become more endurable if employees were allowed prolonged absences. And employers might find it easier to recruit for routine jobs if prospective workers were not forced to make career commitments. In the case of more creative skilled work, it is apparent that we are already moving toward project jobs and more temporary organizational structures.[12] Here, workers will automatically experience junctures between jobs, which may be extended or shortened by personal preference. It can be expected that the transition between jobs or work periods will be smoothed out by regional and national computerized job information and matching facilities. The net effect will be more fluid work scheduling on both a short- and long-run basis.

From the standpoint of management, the feasibility of increasing work-scheduling flexibility has been relatively unexplored. With large, multishift manufacturing industries, for example, its potential is unlimited and highly timely. Such organizations are presently beset by growing worker malaise manifested by work stoppages, excessive absenteeism, and sabotage, which are caused partly by placing workers in highly constrained and boring work without taking individual motivations or tolerances into consideration.[13] Chucking the standard work week and moving totally over to a system of individual work scheduling promise to be a strong antidote. Workers could be asked to submit their preferences and contingency preferences for work hours a few days prior to the beginning of each week. Computers could integrate individual schedules in the way classrooms are now allocated and scheduled in multiversities and airline reservations are made on a national basis. The results might not be perfect, but it is likely that the unmarried twenty-year-old on the assembly line, for instance, would come closer to working the twenty hours a week that he truly wants, and the family man on the same line would get the extra overtime he needs. A contingency work force could be held on call for last-minute scheduling problems, and a probable positive by-product would be more job opportunities for those who need them.

In smaller, more personal work organizations, flexible work scheduling is already relatively common, and there is little reason why it cannot be expanded further. A possible move in this direction would be to make the two-way negotiation of work scheduling a common aspect of the hiring procedure. Today, most people looking for a job assume that they will work about forty hours, five days

[12] Alvin Toffler, *Future Shock* (New York: Random House, 1970), pp. 108–32.
[13] William Serrin, "The Assembly Line," *Atlantic Monthly,* October 1971, pp. 62–74.

a week. In the future prospective employees may be able to discuss their work-scheduling preferences in more detail, necessarily subject to organizational constraints and the complications of reaching mutual agreements. Of course, this would entail extra managerial efforts; however, the results in terms of higher worker morale, decreased turnover, and better job performance would certainly more than compensate.

In sum, work scheduling, as all aspects of contemporary life, is subject to the expanding options made possible by increasing affluence. The ongoing growth of personal earnings makes it likely that increasing numbers of persons will prefer to sacrifice potential income in favor of more free time. But for persons who have worked forty-hour weeks for years, the psychological and economic reorientation to a more leisure-based life-style may be difficult and frightening. Our experiences with forced retirement and sudden severance from work suggest that such realignments of life-styles should be allowed to occur gradually in accord with individual needs. Also in juxtaposition to those deemphasizing their work involvement, others are adjusting to greater workloads or, for one reason or another, need increased earnings. Needs and preferences concerning combinations of work, income, and free time are a highly individual matter. The growing sense of suboptimization concerning the forty-hour week cannot be reduced by instigating a new standard work week. We have reached a point of societal development where it is feasible and desirable to allow increased individualization in all aspects of life. In the case of the work week, this means that we should seek to move toward more work-scheduling flexibility to match individual needs.

Section D

work and education: an emerging synthesis

The purposes of education have broadened and changed greatly throughout history. Education has sought to convey the wisdom and practical discoveries of former generations to the younger generation so that they can avoid the mistakes of the past and build upon the heritage of previously developed resources and knowledge. In one form or another, education has been a basic requirement for the continuity and growth of even the most rudimentary forms of civilization.

Until the twentieth century the educational experiences of most persons took the form of family socialization, a limited amount of elementary schooling, and some form of apprenticeship. Education at the college level was seen primarily as a leisure activity which could be pursued only by persons from the most privileged backgrounds. Today education at the college or technical school level is considered a commonplace preparation for life and work. In the future, work itself will probably become an innovative or exploratory activity requiring continuous "job-related" learning. Advanced or higher education will have progressed from a leisure pursuit to a common preparation for work to work itself. Tomorrow's worker will be increasingly concerned with, in Marshall McLuhan's words, "learning a living."

The evolution of work into an educational activity can be seen in numerous ways. As noted previously, cybernation and technology are gradually assuming routine and predictable work chores. As this trend continues, we find ourselves more and more concerned with exploring and evaluating the unknown frontiers of human existence. Out of this comes a growing prominence of the "knowledge worker," whose job is to discover, integrate, process, and find applications for our constantly exploding reserves of knowledge.

Despite the growing importance of knowledge work, many

complications obscure the relevance of education both as a preparation for work and a work activity unto itself. One such complexity
is evidenced by the emerging debate about the amount and nature
of education that a person truly needs to perform today's work.
The debate stems from the popular assumption during the 1950s
and 1960s that technological advances would raise the skill requirements of future jobs and require the cultivation of a highly educated
labor force.[1] Today this assumption is being challenged. It is true
that new and highly complex forms of work are evolving. However,
hard data gathered during the last two decades present strong arguments that with most work, skill requirements are remaining at the
same level or even declining.[2] The concrete results of these circumstances are becoming evident in the everyday dynamics of the labor
market. The fact is that 80 percent of our jobs require little more
than a high school diploma. Yet we are still sending 60 percent of
our recent high school graduates and increasing proportions of other
age group members to college. Many scholars suggest that the result
is a surplus of educated workers and an unnecessary boosting of
educational requirements for jobs which in reality have not become
more difficult.[3] A case in point is sales clerk jobs which, if anything,
have grown easier yet now require two years of college as opposed
to the two years of high school of a few decades ago.

The natural response to this "educational inflation" is to assume that we are overeducating and should cut back on educational
efforts. The problem, however, is more complex. We have not over-
educated, rather we have failed to take advantage of our highest
potentials and skills. We have educated millions of persons, height-
ened the skill levels of our labor force, and increased the general
capacity to learn. Yet, instead of finding ways to utilize our educational strengths to improve conditions, we have sought to employ
educated workers in old types of routine work. We have not created
jobs allowing our technicians and social scientists to develop new
ways to reduce and automate factory work but have forced them
to work on factory assembly lines. We have acted correctly in in-

[1] Burton Clark, *Educating the Expert Society* (San Francisco: Chandler
Publishing Co., 1962).

[2] James R. Bright, "Does Automation Raise Skill Requirements," in *Exploring the Dimensions of the Manpower Revolution*, U.S. Senate, Subcommittee
on Employment and Manpower (Washington, D.C.: Government Printing Office,
1964), pp. 558–80; and Ivar Berg, *Education and Jobs: The Great Training Rob-
bery* (New York: Praeger Publishers, 1970).

[3] Eli Ginzberg, "The Sixties-Manpower Horizons: Machines Versus Men,"
in *Exploring the Dimensions of the Manpower Revolution*, pp. 453–60.

creasing our educational opportunities, but we have fallen short in our use of educated manpower.

In the immediate future it will be increasingly important to recognize that education and work are becoming synonymous. Exploring and learning will ultimately become our primary productive activities. Further, we will find exploring and learning becoming central concerns of all aspects of life. As a result, new institutions and concepts will have to be developed to facilitate the integration of work, leisure, and education within the total contexts of our lives.

In the first selection of this section philosopher-technologist Marshall McLuhan illustrates the growing similarities between work and education. He envisions the development of global technological systems which will catapult tomorrow's society into a series of circular and ongoing information "loops." As these systems develop, our primary responsibilities will entail the creation, communication, and integration of information. In his famous nonlinear writing style, McLuhan presents many innovative spin-off ideas which make what he has written worth a little extra time and consideration. The second selection excerpts a report of the Conference on Educational Priorities conducted under the auspices of the U.S. Office of Education. The report provides a "nuts and bolts" prediction of the kind of fluid educational systems that must be developed in the future.

Chapter 10

learning a living

Marshall McLuhan

A newspaper headline recently read, "Little Red Schoolhouse Dies When Good Road Built." One-room schools, with all subjects being taught to all grades at the same time, simply dissolve when better transportation permits specialized spaces and specialized teaching. At the extreme of speeded-up movement, however, specialism of space and subject disappears once more. With automation, it is not only jobs that disappear, and complex roles that reappear. Centuries of specialist stress in pedagogy and in the arrangement of data now end with the instantaneous retrieval of information made possible by electricity. Automation is information and it not only ends jobs in the world of work, it ends subjects in the world of learning. It does not end the world of learning. The future of work consists of learning a living in the automation age. This is a familiar pattern in electric technology in general. It ends the old dichotomies between culture and technology, between art and commerce, and between work and leisure. Whereas in the mechanical age of fragmentation leisure had been the absence of work, or mere idleness, the reverse is true in the electric age. As the age of information demands the simultaneous use of all our faculties, we discover that we are most at leisure when we are most intensely involved, very much as with the artists in all ages.

In terms of the industrial age, it can be pointed out that the difference between the previous mechanical age and the new electric age appears in the different kinds of inventories. Since electricity, inventories are made up not so much of goods in storage as of materials in continuous process of transformation at spatially removed sites. For electricity not only gives primacy to *process*, whether in making or in learning, but it makes independent the source of energy from the location of the process. In entertainment media, we speak of this fact as "mass media" because the source of the program and the process of experiencing it are independent in space, yet simultaneous in time. In industry this basic fact causes the scientific revolution that is called "automation" or "cybernation."

In education the conventional division of the curriculum into subjects is already as outdated as the medieval trivium and quadrivium after the Renaissance. Any subject taken in depth at once relates to other subjects. Arithmetic in grade three or nine, when taught in terms of number theory, symbolic logic, and cultural history, ceases to be mere practice in problems. Continued in their present patterns of fragmented unrelation, our school curricula will insure a citizenry unable to understand the cybernated world in which they live.

Most scientists are quite aware that since we have acquired some knowledge of electricity it is not possible to speak of atoms as pieces of matter. Again, as more is known about electrical "discharges" and energy, there is less and less tendency to speak of electricity as a thing that "flows" like water through a wire, or is "contained" in a battery. Rather, the tendency is to speak of electricity as painters speak of space; namely, that it is a variable condition that involves the special positions of two or more bodies. There is no longer any tendency to speak of electricity as "contained" in anything. Painters have long known that objects are not contained in space, but that they generate their own spaces. It was the dawning awareness of this in the mathematical world a century ago that enabled Lewis Carroll, the Oxford mathematician, to contrive *Alice in Wonderland,* in which times and spaces are neither uniform nor continuous, as they had seemed to be since the arrival of Renaissance perspective. As for the speed of light, that is merely the speed of total causality.

It is a principal aspect of the electric age that it establishes a global network that has much of the character of our central nervous system. Our central nervous system is not merely an electric network, but it constitutes a single unified field of experience. As biologists point out, the brain is the interacting place where all kinds of impressions and experiences can be exchanged and translated, enabling us to *react to the world as a whole.* Naturally, when electric technology comes into play, the utmost variety and extent of operations in industry and society quickly assume a unified posture. Yet this organic unity of interprocess that electromagnetism inspires in the most diverse and specialized areas and organs of action is quite the opposite of organization in a mechanized society. Mechanization of any process is achieved by fragmentation, beginning with the mechanization of writing by movable types, which has been called the "monofracture of manufacture."

The electric telegraph, when crossed with typography, created the strange new form of the modern newspaper. Any page of the telegraph press is a surrealistic mosaic of bits of "human interest" in vivid interaction. Such was the art form of Chaplin and the early silent movies. Here, too, an extreme speed-up of mechanization, an assembly line of still shots on celluloid, led to a strange reversal. The movie mechanism, aided by the electric light, created the illusion of organic form and movement as much as a fixed position had created the illusion of perspective on a flat surface five hundred years before.

The same thing happens less superficially when the electric principle crosses the mechanical lines of industrial organization. Automation retains only as much of the mechanical character as the motorcar kept of the forms of the horse and the carriage. Yet people discuss automation as if we had not passed the oat barrier, and as if the horse-vote at the next poll would sweep away the automation regime.

Automation is not an extension of the mechanical principles of fragmentation and separation of operations. It is rather the invasion of the mechanical world by the instantaneous character of electricity. That is why those involved in automation insist that it is a way of thinking, as much as it is a way of doing. Instant synchronization of numerous operations has ended the old mechanical pattern of setting up operations in lineal sequence. The assembly line has gone the way of the stag line. Nor is it just the lineal and sequential aspect of mechanical analysis that has been erased by the electric speed-up and exact synchronizing of information that is automation.

Automation or cybernation deals with all the units and components of the industrial and marketing process exactly as radio or TV combine the individuals in the audience into new interprocess. The new kind of interrelation in both industry and entertainment is the result of the electric instant speed. Our new electric technology now extends the instant processing of knowledge by interrelation that has long occurred within our central nervous system. It is that same speed that constitutes "organic unity" and ends the mechanical age that had gone into high gear with Gutenberg. Automation brings in real "mass production," not in terms of size, but of an instant inclusive embrace. Such is also the character of "mass media." They are an indication, not of the size of their audiences, but of the fact that everybody becomes involved in them at the same time. Thus commodity industries under automation share the same structural character of the entertainment industries in the degree that both approximate the condition of instant information. Automation affects not just production, but every phase of consumption and marketing; for the consumer becomes producer in the automation circuit, quite as much as the reader of the mosaic telegraph press makes his own news, or just *is* his own news.

But there is a component in the automation story that is as basic as tactility to the TV image. It is the fact that, in any automatic machine, or galaxy of machines and functions, the generation and transmission of power is quite separate from the work operation that uses the power. The same is true in all servomechanist structures that involve feedback. The source of energy is separate from the process of translation of information, or the applying of knowledge. This is obvious in the telegraph, where the energy and channel are quite independent of whether the written code is French or German. The same separation of power and process obtains in automated industry, or in "cybernation." The electric energy can be applied indifferently and quickly to many kinds of tasks.

Such was never the case in the mechanical systems. The power and the work done were always in direct relation, whether it was hand and hammer, water and wheel, horse and cart, or steam and piston. Electricity brought a strange elasticity in this matter, much as light itself illuminates a total field and does not dictate what shall be done. The same light can make possible a multiplicity of tasks, just as with electric power. Light is a nonspecialist kind of energy or power that is identical with information and knowledge. Such is also the relation of electricity to automation, since both energy and information can be applied in a great variety of ways.

Grasp of this fact is indispensable to the understanding of the electronic age, and of automation in particular. Energy and production now tend to fuse with information and learning. Marketing and consumption tend to become one with learning, enlightenment, and the intake of information. This is all part of the electric *implosion* that now follows or succeeds the centuries of *explosion* and increasing specialism. The electronic age is literally one of illumination. Just as light is at once energy and information, so electric automation unites production, consumption, and learning in an inextricable process. For this reason, teachers are already the largest employee group in the U.S. economy, and may well become the *only* group.

The very same process of automation that causes a withdrawal of the present work force from industry causes learning itself to become the principal kind of production and consumption. Hence the folly of alarm about unemployment. Paid learning is already becoming both the dominant employment and the source of new wealth in our society. This is the new *role* for men in society, whereas the older mechanistic idea of "jobs," or fragmented tasks and specialist slots for "workers," becomes meaningless under automation.

It has often been said by engineers that, as information levels rise, almost any sort of material can be adapted to any sort of use. This principle is the key to the understanding of electric automation. In the case of electricity, as energy for production becomes independent of the work operation, there is not only the speed that makes for total and organic interplay, but there is, also, the fact that electricity is sheer information that, in actual practice, illuminates all it touches. Any process that approaches instant interrelation of a total field tends to raise itself to the level of conscious awareness, so that computers seem to "think." In fact, they are highly specialized at present, and quite lacking in the full process of interrelation that makes for consciousness. Obviously, they can be made to simulate the process of consciousness, just as our electric global networks now begin to simulate the condition of our central nervous system. But a conscious computer would still be one that was an extension of our consciousness, as a telescope is an extension of our eyes, or as a ventriloquist's dummy is an extension of the ventriloquist.

Automation certainly assumes the servomechanism and the computer. That is to say, it assumes electricity as store and expediter of information. These traits of store, or "memory," and accelerator are the basic features of any medium of communication whatever. In the case of electricity, it is not corporeal substance that is stored or moved, but perception and information. As for technological acceleration, it now approaches the speed of light. All nonelectric media had merely hastened things a bit. The wheel, the road, the ship, the airplane, and even the space rocket are utterly lacking in the character of instant movement. Is it strange, then, that electricity should confer on all previous human organization a completely new character? The very toil of man now becomes a kind of enlightenment. As unfallen Adam in the Garden of Eden was appointed the task of the contemplation and naming of creatures, so with automation. We have now only to name and program a process or a product in order for it to be accomplished. Is it not rather like the case of Al Capp's Schmoos? One had only to look at a Schmoo and think longingly of pork chops or caviar, and the Schmoo ecstatically transformed itself into the object of desire. Automation brings us into the world of the Schmoo. The custom-built supplants the mass-produced.

Let us, as the Chinese say, move our chairs closer to the fire and see what we are saying. The electric changes associated with automation have nothing to do with ideologies or social programs. If they had, they could be delayed or controlled. Instead, the technological extension of our central nervous system that we call the electric media began more than a century ago, subliminally. Subliminal have been the effects. Subliminal they remain. At no period in human culture have men understood the psychic mechanisms involved in invention and technology. Today it is the instant speed of electric information that, for the first time, permits easy recognition of the patterns and the formal contours of change and development. The entire world, past and present, now reveals itself to us like a growing plant in an enormously accelerated movie. Electric speed is synonymous with light and with the understanding of causes. So, with the use of electricity in previously mechanized situations, men easily discover causal connections and patterns that were quite unobservable at the slower rates of mechanical change. If we play backward the long development of literacy and printing and their effects on social experience and organization, we can easily see how these forms brought about that high degree of social uniformity and homogeneity of society that is indispensable for mechanical industry. Play them backward, and we get just that shock of unfamiliarity in the familiar that is necessary for the understanding of the life of forms. Electricity compels us to play our mechanical development backward, for it reverses much of that development. Mechanization depends on the breaking up of processes into homogenized but unrelated bits. Electricity unifies these fragments once more because its speed of operation requires a high degree of interdependence among all phases of any operation. It is this electric speed-up and interdependence that has ended the assembly line in industry.

This same need for organic interrelation, brought in by the electric speed of synchronization, now requires us to perform, industry-by-industry, and country-by-country, exactly the same organic interrelating that was first effected in the individual automated unit. Electric speed requires organic structuring of the global economy quite as much as early mechanization by print and by road led to the acceptance of national unity. Let us not forget that nationalism was a mighty invention and revolution that, in the Renaissance, wiped out many of the local regions and loyalties. It was a revolution achieved almost entirely by the speed-up of information by means of uniform movable types. Nationalism cut across most of the traditional power and cultural groupings that had slowly grown up in various regions. Multi-nationalisms had long deprived Europe of its economic unity. The Common Market came to it only with the Second War. War is accelerated social change, as an explosion is an accelerated chemical reaction and movement of matter. With electric speeds governing industry and social life, explosion in the sense of crash development becomes normal. On the other hand, the old-fashioned kind of "war" becomes as impracticable as playing hop-scotch with bulldozers. Organic interdependence means that disruption of any part of the organism can prove fatal to the whole. Every industry has had to "rethink through" (the awkwardness of this phrase betrays the painfulness of the process), function by function, its place in the economy. But automation forces not only industry and town planners, but government and even education, to come into some relation to social facts.

The various military branches have had to come into line with automation very quickly. The unwieldy mechanical forms of military organization have gone. Small teams of experts have replaced the citizen armies of yesterday even faster than they have taken over the reorganization of industry. Uniformly trained and homogenized citizenry, so long in preparation and so necessary to a mechanized society, is becoming quite a burden and problem to an automated society, for automation and electricity require depth approaches in all fields and at all times. Hence the sudden rejection of standardized goods and scenery and living and education in America since the Second War. It is a switch imposed by electric technology in general, and by the TV image in particular.

Automation was first felt and seen on a large scale in the chemical industries of gas, coal, oil, and metallic ores. The large changes in these operations made possible by electric energy have now, by means of the computer, begun to invade every kind of white-collar and management area. Many people, in consequence, have begun to look on the whole of society as a single unified machine for creating wealth. Such has been the normal outlook of the stockbroker, manipulating shares and information with the cooperation of the electric media of press, radio, telephone, and teletype. But the peculiar and abstract manipulation of information as a means of creating wealth is no longer a monopoly of the stockbroker. It is now shared by every engineer and by the entire communications industries. With electricity as energizer and synchronizer, all aspects of production, consumption, and organization become incidental to communications. The very idea of communication as interplay is inherent in the electrical, which combines both energy and information in its intensive manifold.

Anybody who begins to examine the patterns of automation finds that perfecting the individual machine by making it automatic involves "feedback." That means introducing an information loop or circuit, where before there had been merely a one-way flow or mechanical sequence. Feedback is the end of the lineality that came into the Western world with the alphabet and the continuous forms of Euclidean space. Feedback or dialogue between the mechanism and its environment brings a further weaving of individual machines into a galaxy of such machines throughout the entire plant. There follows a still further weaving of individual plants and factories into the entire industrial matrix of materials and services of a culture. Naturally, this last stage encounters the entire world of policy, since to deal with the whole industrial complex as an organic system affects employment, security, education, and politics, demanding full understanding in advance of coming structural change. There is no room for witless assumptions and subliminal factors in such electrical and instant organizations.

As artists began a century ago to construct their works backward, *starting with the effect,* so now with industry and planning. In general, electric speed-up requires complete knowledge of ultimate effects. Mechanical speed-ups, however radical in their reshaping of personal and social life, still were allowed to happen sequentially. Men could, for the most part, get through a normal life span on the basis of a single set of skills. That is not at all the case with electric speed-up. The acquiring of new basic knowledge and skill by senior executives in middle age is one of the most common needs and harrowing facts of electric technology. The senior executives, or "big wheels," as they are archaically and ironically designated, are among the hardest pressed and most persistently harassed groups in human history. Electricity has not only demanded ever deeper knowledge and faster interplay, but has made the harmonizing of production schedules as rigorous as that demanded of the members of a large symphony orchestra. And the satisfactions are just as few for the big executives as for the symphonists, since a player in a big orchestra can hear nothing of the music that reaches the audience. He gets only noise.

The result of electric speed-up in industry at large is the creation of intense sensitivity to the interrelation and interprocess of the whole, so as to call for ever-new types of organization and talent. Viewed from the old perspectives of the machine age, this electric network of plants and processes seems brittle and tight. In fact, it is not mechanical, and it does begin to develop the sensitivity and pliability of the human organism. But it also demands the same varied nutriment and nursing as the animal organism.

With the instant and complex interprocesses of the organic form, automated industry also acquires the power of adaptability to multiple uses. A machine set up for the automatic production of electric bulbs represents a combination of processes that were previously managed by several machines. With a single attendant, it can run as continuously as a tree in its intake and output. But, unlike the tree, it has a built-in system of jigs and fixtures that can be shifted to cause the machine to turn out a whole range of products from radio tubes and glass tumblers to Christmas-tree ornaments. Although an automated plant is almost like a tree in respect to the continuous intake and output, it is a tree that can change from oak to maple to walnut as required. It is part of the automation or electric logic that specialism is no longer limited to just one specialty. The automatic machine may work in a specialist way, but it is not limited to one line. As with our hands and fingers that are capable of many tasks, the automatic unit incorporates a power of adaptation that was quite lacking in the pre-electric and mechanical stage of technology. As *anything* becomes more complex, it becomes less specialized. Man is more complex and less specialized than a dinosaur. The older mechanical operations were designed to be more efficient as they became larger and more specialized. The electric and automated unit, however, is quite otherwise. A new automatic machine for making automobile tailpipes is about the size of two or three office desks. The computer control panel is the size of a lectern. It has in it no dies, no fixtures, no settings of any kind, but rather certain general-purpose things like grippers, benders, and advancers. On this machine, starting with lengths of ordinary pipe, it is possible to make eighty different kinds of tailpipe in succession, as rapidly, as easily, and as cheaply as it is to make eighty of the same kind. And the characteristic of electric automation is all in this direction of return to the general-purpose handicraft flexibility that our own hands possess. The programming can now include endless changes of program. It is the electric feedback, or dialogue pattern, of the automatic and computer-programmed "machine" that marks it off from the older mechanical principle of one-way movement.

This computer offers a model that has the characteristics shared by all automation. From the point of intake of materials to the output of the finished product, the operations tend to be independently, as well as interdependently, automatic. The synchronized concert of operations is under the control of gauges and instruments that can be varied from the control-panel boards that are themselves electronic. The material of intake is relatively uniform in shape, size, and chemical properties, as likewise the material of the output. But the processing under these conditions permits use of the highest level of capacity for any needed period. It is, as compared with the older machines, the difference between an oboe in an orchestra and the same tone on an electronic music instrument. With the electronic music instrument, any tone can be made available in any intensity and for any length of time. Note that the older symphony orchestra was, by comparison, a machine of separate instruments that *gave the effect of organic unity*. With the electronic instrument, one *starts* with organic unity as an immediate fact of perfect synchronization. This makes the attempt to create the effect of organic unity quite pointless. Electronic music must seek other goals.

Such is also the harsh logic of industrial automation. All that we had previously achieved mechanically by great exertion and co-ordination can now be done electrically without effort. Hence the specter of joblessness and propertylessness in the electric age. Wealth and work become information factors, and totally new structures are needed to run a business or relate it to social needs and markets. With the electric technology, the new kinds of instant interdependence and interprocess that take over production also enter the market and social organizations. For this reason, markets and education designed to cope with the products of servile toil and mechanical production are no longer adequate. Our education has long ago acquired the fragmentary and piecemeal character of mechanism. It is now under increasing pressure to acquire the depth and interrelation that are indispensable in the all-at-once world of electric organization.

Paradoxically, automation makes liberal education mandatory. The electric age of servomechanisms suddenly releases men from the mechanical and specialist servitude of the preceding machine age. As the machine and the motorcar released the horse and projected it onto the plane of entertainment, so does automation with men. We are suddenly threatened with a liberation that taxes our inner resources of self-employment and imaginative participation in society. This would seem to be a fate that calls men to the role of artist in society. It has the effect of making most people realize how much they had come to depend on the fragmentalized and repetitive routines of the mechanical era. Thousands of years ago man, the nomadic food-gatherer, had taken up positional, or relatively sedentary, tasks. He began to specialize. The development of writing and printing were major stages of that process. They were supremely specialists in separating the roles of knowledge from the roles of action, even though at times it could appear that "the pen is mightier than the sword." But with electricity and automation, the technology of fragmented processes suddenly fused with the human dialogue and the need for over-all consideration of human unity. Men are suddenly nomadic gatherers of knowledge, nomadic as never before, informed as never before, free from fragmentary specialism as never before—but also involved in the total social process as never before; since with electricity we extend our central nervous system globally, instantly interrelating every human experience. Long accustomed to such a state in stock-market news or front-page sensations, we can grasp the meaning of this new dimension more readily when it is pointed out that it is possible to "fly" unbuilt airplanes on computers. The specifications of a plane can be programmed and the plane tested under a variety of extreme conditions before it has left the drafting board. So with new products and new organizations of many kinds. We can now, by computer, deal with complex social needs with the same architectural certainty that we previously attempted in private housing. Industry as a whole has become the unit of reckoning, and so with society, politics, and education as wholes.

Electric means of storing and moving information with speed and precision make the largest units quite as manageable as small ones. Thus the automation of a plant or of an entire industry offers a small model of the changes that must occur in society from the same electric technology. Total interdependence is the starting fact. Nevertheless, the range of choice in design, stress, and goal within that total field of electromagnetic interprocess is very much greater than it ever could have been under mechanization.

Since electric energy is independent of the place or kind of work-operation, it creates patterns of decentralism and diversity in the work to be done. This is a logic that appears plainly enough in the difference between firelight and electric light, for example. Persons grouped around a fire or candle for warmth or light are less able to pursue independent thoughts, or even tasks, than people supplied with electric light. In the same way, the social and educational patterns latent in automation are those of self-employment and artistic autonomy. Panic about automation as a threat of uniformity on a world scale is the projection into the future of mechanical standardization and specialism, which are now past.

Chapter 11

the learning society:
institutions to integrate
work and education

Report of the Conference
on Educational Priorities

[Humanity] has a wide range of needs stemming from the most common physiological necessities to the most individualized drives for self-fulfillment. All human endeavor appears to deal with finding and applying new, better, or alternative strategies for satisfying these needs. The individual involved in this process is essentially concerned with the objectives of recognizing his own needs, understanding the nature of his environment, and learning to interact positively with his environment to satisfy his needs. Essentially, this is the growth process. It deals with enlarging, scaling down, and adjusting one's conception of his needs and what can and must be done to satisfy them. In social or moral terms, the two aspects of the growth process might be described as personal freedom and responsibility. In systems theory, they might be termed objectives and constraints.

The growth process essentially entails mastering the understanding and application of a given set of need satisfying strategies, envisioning and attempting to apply a new and presumed better set of need satisfying strategies, and evaluating the success of the new set of strategies. Fritz Perles and Carl Rogers both suggest that the continuation of this process will cause an individual to progress from dependence upon environmental support to self-support. Essentially, the growth process leads a person to a mature understanding of both himself and his environment.

The dynamics and direction of growth is intricately related to education and learning. Indeed, it is not presumptuous to assume that both growth and education are and should be the same. Ideally

"The Learning Society: Institutions to Integrate Work and Education" (editor's title). Abridged from U.S. Office of Education, *Student Hopes for Education in the Later 20th Century: A Statement of the Conference on Educational Priorities* (Washington, D.C., 1970), pp. 21–23, 30–58, 65–66.

growth and *education* should promote every type and intensity of human experience at both individual and social levels within the limitations of certain social and environmental constraints. . . . This approach is [based on] . . . the belief that a variety of freely chosen experiences will ultimately cause a person to develop the self-control and internal responsibility needed to interact positively with his environment. . . .

A PROJECTED EDUCATIONAL SYSTEM

[In these times] it is commonly claimed that current educational institutions are neither meeting the needs of "students" nor our general society. There seems to be a decreasing need for the graduates of our schools, and "students" of all ages remark about the personal and occupational irrelevance of our educational system. In the case of work, the relation between school and opportunities for employment is becoming increasingly indirect and even counter-effective. Clearly new ways must be found to better integrate work and education within the context of the realities of today and the probabilities of tomorrow. The changes demanded by these times promise to be massive. Indeed, they entail a major re-definition of education that will lead to fundamental alterations of the content, process, and resources of our educational institutions. . . .

Process

The nature of the educational and growth process appears to follow re-occurring cycles of expansion and contraction. In one way or another, every aspect of life seems to follow the process of investment, consumption, over-consumption, and finally a return to the need for more investment. The ultimate effect is a growing ability to produce what is consumed or learn to do without it. The latter case causes degeneration and death unless new opportunities are found and the individual or society has the freedom to pursue them. At this point a choice of numerous, leisure, educational, or productive opportunities can produce a rejuvenative and renewing effect upon both an individual and a society.

The prospect of creating such renewing experiences approaches the problem of achieving widespread human fulfillment for an entire society. This is a delicate and in many cases dangerous endeavor. For the needs and satisfactions of one individual may be an anathema to another. As such, the problem of optimizing the growth and educational process becomes one of creating a situation which allows men the freedom and opportunity for the orderly and positive exploration of every conceivable aspect of their natures within certain minimal constraints set by their social and ecological surroundings.

The prospect of giving individuals of all ages and social backgrounds relevant self-renewing education is awesome. This calls for a tremendous expansion and diversification of current educational opportunities and a vast reduction of current restrictive practices curtailing the learner's ability to change and experiment with his educational activities. Essentially, education must teach persons how to learn and keep learning. Emphasis must be placed on learning the learning process as well as the content.

The process of education must allow the integration of all content so that the learner can develop a holistic conception of all that he learns. Such a holistic approach will not only allow an individual to relate himself better to his environment but also promote a wider and deeper level of social consciousness and responsibility. Such an approach means that knowledge cannot be separated and kept in "disciplinary" or "classroom" boxes. Rather the learner must be able to jump freely from one subject to another as each subject seems relevant to his own needs.

Basically, this means that learners cannot be captivated by a teacher, school, classroom, grades, degrees, courses, or particular academic disciplines. This sweeping proposal for educational freedom might be criticized on the basis that the result of such a process would be a lack of discipline and valuable content.

This criticism overlooks the increasing evidence that human beings develop their own self-disciplines to pursue their interests and that there are basic disciplines such as communication, non-violence, rational problem solving, and health care which are intrinsically valuable and commonly sought traits for both the individual and society. As an individual learns about himself, his environment, and the alternative need satisfying strategies which are mutually acceptable to both himself and his environment, he will learn how to make an optimal social contribution with his individual qualities. Yet at the same time, the individual will be more likely to retain his motivation and ability to grow.

Another objection to freeing the educational process is the fear that students will make mistakes which are harmful to themselves and others. This is a pertinent reservation. First, within certain specifications, mistakes and failures are often one of the most effective teaching devices. Real experiences, when successful, give a person motivation and self-confidence. Mistakes, on the other hand, make a person question, communicate, and develop problem solving abilities. Both are important. If a child eats dirt and finds it distasteful, he has learned something real and no real harm has been done. However, if he jumps off a two-story building to fly or hits another child with a baseball bat to see the reaction, that is another matter. This brings us to the second point.

The prevention of injury and costly mistakes may not always be avoidable. Yet they should be avoided as much as possible. This can be done in two ways. First, by providing a minimum level of supervision and guidance relevant to a given developmental level which will prevent undue accidents. Second, by providing positive alternatives which will provide a more effective need satisfying activity than another undesirable approach. Young children should have some type of supervision to keep them from jumping off buildings or eating poison. Additionally, the child or adult who has a tendency to harm or "bully" others should have an alternative course available which would be more rewarding for himself and those around him.

Basically, we are saying that education must be a feeling experience as much as a cognitive or abstract thinking process. Education and life should be directly equated and learners should be able to flow easily between the various facets of life in a way which is personally relevant. The learner who wants to work with wood should go to a carpenter's or sculptor's workplace. The learner who wants to understand political science should be involved in politics. This is not to say that books and the opportunity for abstract thinking have no place but rather that they must be mingled and mutually reinforced with experience. People think and deal abstractly under two circumstances. First, when they experience some failure or hardship which requires a reorientation of their need satisfying strategies. Second, when they must make a choice between two or more real or potential alternatives. The educational process must provide the opportunity for both real experience and detached thought.

Resources

For years uniformity and inflexibility have characterized many areas of American education. Today such traits are neither desirable nor necessary. They can and must be replaced by educational systems which promote expanded choice, individualism, and equality. This will require a major reorganization of educational personnel, facilities, and general resources.

Such a reorganization is not simple. Essentially, it calls for the development and usage of educational resources in a way which allows the integration of education into every aspect of society and life. In order to accomplish this, resources must be developed and used in compliance with three new principles of education. First, education and learning need not follow any generally accepted time or curricular progression. Second, education and learning should not be restricted or made more available to any particular age of social group. Third, academic scholarship and vocational training should not be considered "more educational" or better learning experiences than general life experiences such as work and leisure.

If educational resources are to be used in a way which promotes these goals, then they cannot be compartmentalized into a school building apart from the real world. Rather, they must be readily available to all persons and used in a way which will not force learners to remain within a given facility or situation defined by someone else as "educational."

1. Educational Personnel. Educational personnel [are] directly or indirectly involved in providing learning experiences. If these learning experiences are to be expansive and unconfining, they should offer a wide range of options, be available to the free self-choice of the learner, and be presented in a way which allows individualized creativity and growth. In order to promote such learning experiences, educational personnel must develop the ability to facilitate the growth of others without "forcing" their own values and expectations upon them. They must provide alternatives for the learner without forcing them to choose between them. Put in another way, they should show "a" way, not "the" way to do things. In this sense, they should function as facilitators rather than directors of education. This requires educational personnel to be allowed and able to direct their concern toward the total learning environment and total people rather than [toward] the infeasible burden of maintaining inflexible authority or the role and image of an expert.

It is common to view educational personnel in terms of the teacher at the core of the learning process backed by supporting personnel. This view is obsolete. Today's educational systems must place the individual learner at the core of the learning experience. This can be done by forgetting the notion of a central school or classroom and recognizing that the learner is both willing and capable of moving himself to the educational resources which he considers most personally relevant. Such a learner centered educational process suggests a fundamental re-orientation of the role of the teacher and his supporting personnel.

An educational system which optimizes choice, individualism and equality will shift more toward a counselor-participation orientation rather than a teacher-classroom situation. There will still be teachers, but they would not direct education. Instead, they would be available to individuals and groups for information and mutual problem solving efforts.

Basically, these teacher-counselors must have three fundamental traits. First, they must have something to communicate. Second, they must know how to communicate. Third, they must be motivated to communicate and be able to motivate others to communicate.

These three functions are intricately related to communication. Studies have shown that communication can only be optimized on a horizontal basis or under conditions of equality between the participants. By equality, we mean that no one side will have the power or authority to declare the other wrong by decree and that each party have the ability to withdraw from interaction without penalty. This does not mean that the teacher-counselor may not know more about a given topic. Rather the weight of his views will depend upon his ability to communicate, and the validity and value of his comments to the particular learner. Under these circumstances, the teacher-counselor would have to rely upon what Robert Theobald calls "sapiential authority." Such authority relies on the value and validity of one's knowledge and communicative ability, not his formal position or coercive influence.

The growth of "sapiential authority" among educational personnel should have two effects. First, it ensures that a person's right to teach is determined by whether anyone will listen to him as much as by credentials or formal position. Second, it ensures that both teacher and learner must meet at points and levels of common understanding. Failures to meet at levels of common understanding will be mutually unrewarding for both teacher and learner and therefore avoided by both parties.

Credentials will most likely become substantially less important for educational personnel in the future. Certification, via experience or degree, may retain importance in determining a person's proficiency in an area of knowledge. However, a person's teaching abilities should be determined by actual teaching experience or apprenticeships rather than by credentials. Such a de-emphasis of credentials should have the dual effect of reducing the number of unsuited teachers by self- and learner selection and increasing the potential manpower available for teaching. Matched by adequate facilities, these conditions should allow learners to seek out and stay with *people* who *can* teach them something rather than be forced to learn from *teachers* who are *supposed* to be able to teach them something.

2. *Facilities.* Time and time again students have expressed substantial disillusionment with the existing school "system." Schools have been discussed as legal, social, financial prisons for which there was no alternative or escape. Rational discussion of these complaints [gives] them further legitimacy. For example, . . . individuali[ty is] both minimized and degraded by "common" standards and a lack of alternative programs. Equality [is] undermined by ethnic segregation and the low "prestige" of certain programs such as vocational training. Choice [is] minimized by basic requirements, a lack of alternative educational programs, and mandatory attendance. [These observations point to] a central theme . . . : the idea of one school system [is] obsolete, suboptimal, and destructive to the creativity and enthusiasm of most students. The conclusion— efforts must be made to develop numerous school systems or educational options.

The initial prospect of developing numerous school systems is enough to frighten even the most open-minded pragmatist. However, this prospect is not as staggering as it may first seem. Indeed, the basic facilities for such alternatives exist in large part already. One has only to look at the daily newspaper and magazines or listen to the radio or the next door neighbor to find many of them. A brief skim of the daily news will reveal hundreds of educational opportunities: private training institutes, motion pictures and television, apprenticeships, "free schools," museums, art galleries, libraries, local sites of interest, and community recreational programs. For example:

1. This summer the *Berkeley Tribe* carried an article which listed 16 new alternative schools that were evolving in the San Francisco area of California.

2. The *Washington Post* carries a daily column listing many private training institutes which are available for persons to learn a skill such as computer programming, accounting, or electronics. There are many such advertisements.

3. Even the most common life activities can be used as effective learning experiences. Moving between different ethnic and socio-economic groups within one city could provide valuable sociological

insights. The "Apartments for Rent" column of any common classified ad section provide a start for this type of experience.

4. Both popular and art films provide a powerful educational tool both on and off the campus. This tool should be utilized more.

5. Travel, both extended and local, offers one of the most effective educational experiences available. Schools should use more of the facilities available to them. Likewise, so should individuals.

6. A great deal can be learned by learning to use a new tool or facility. The stimulation of having a new object at one's disposal, such as a car, set of skis, or a common hammer, can be an effective growth situation.

There are a million "educational" experiences in everyday life. There are opportunities such as travel to Europe, moving to a new location, changing one's job, or buying and wearing new and different clothes, to name just a few. In the broadest sense of the word, everything around one offers a unique and stimulating educational experience if one still possesses his motivation and curiosity.

In a more traditional sense, there is a need to provide specific educational facilities for basic human skills such as reading and arithmetic, as well as highly specialized and intricate skills such as medicine or advanced electrical technology. In these areas it is necessary to provide educational facilities. Yet these facilities need not be a part of a linear or [coordinated] "school system." Alternative facilities might be developed for these purposes. To a degree this is already happening with the emerging "free school" system. With or without government support, it can be expected that this trend will grow.

Matched by proper supporting resources, such alternative educational opportunities would enhance equality and mutual human respect by destroying the myth of "a way" to success. At the same time, it would greatly expand the opportunities for choice and individualism by leaving educational . . . decisions to the participating individual. . . .

The major problem is not whether the educational opportunities are available or possible, but rather whether people can obtain the resources to use them and find out about them. The choice is already existent, or easily possible. The potential already exists for a *non-school educational system* or a "learning society." The problem is finding a way to use it.

There are two fundamental problems with a non-school educational system. The first is the necessity to develop a means of developing and maintaining community. In many ways [this first] problem is solved by the growing dissolution of traditional barriers and disciplines which have caused malcommunication and even social polarization due to cumbersome stereotypes originating in many cases from early education. A society and educational system that would allow a man, or a woman, to study both medicine and carpentry at the same time could not help but facilitate the respect and understanding of diverse "life styles."

The second problem stems from the necessity to develop an effective means to inform persons of all the opportunities that are available to them [and provide needed testing and certification mechanisms]. Persons must have adequate opportunity to become aware of the existing and prospective alternatives to their current life and educational activities. Knowledge of alternatives would facilitate the continual integration of society along multi-dimensional bases. This leads to the necessity to develop some type of open community information center.

Community information centers might be set up as multi-purpose facilities designed to serve the functions of a library, film center, museum, special training facilities, voluntary competency testing service, and recreation center. It might provide information about both local community opportunities as well as be tied into a national computer bank which would allow a person to find out about national and international opportunities. Opportunities should be broadly defined to include work, leisure, and educational information. Information should be both general and specific according to the desires of the inquirer and not subject to censorship. Such information centers have been set up as experiments in the United States and used more extensively in other nations such as Sweden. They could be immeasurably valuable as long as they are freely accessible, voluntary, and unrestrictive in information made available.[1]

3. Choice Supporting Resources for the Individual. The ability of a student to choose and influence the type and nature of his educational experiences is intricately related to the development of individualism as a growing person and his equality as a student and member of society. The ability to choose life and educational alternatives is dependent upon two fundamental factors. First, an individual must have some realistic recognition of his own needs which can serve as a choice making criterion. Second, the individual must

[1] [In cases where certification and competency are needed, those learning centers could provide individually scheduled testing service upon request. In areas of highly specialized learning, a variety of extraordinary testing mechanisms could be used.—Ed.]

have potential choices and the ability to pursue them. Essentially, there must be choice supporting resources to support alternatives and the maintenance needs of the participating individuals. Although an individual's recognition of his needs and directions is not insignificant, the adequacy of choice supporting resources is the most pressing choice making constraint for most persons. Choice supporting resources may take the form of available facilities and programs or personal resources. Personal resources are most likely to provide the widest choice making potential for the individual. Within the existing monetary exchange system, a large and frequently critical facet of personal resources takes some form of money. In the area of personal monetary resources, there are numerous existing and proposed programs which approach or satisfy the optimal conditions for personal monetary resources.

One optimal proposal for personal monetary resources takes the form of a *guaranteed income* of adequate size which is provided as an unalterable social right and free from regulations on usage. Such a program, tempered with parental or guardian influences in the cases of children of early ages, would both free all persons from the indignity and paralyzing hardships of poverty and provide leeway for personal growth and experience in areas most relevant and satisfying to the individual. The specifics of the guaranteed income proposal are varied and elaborate. . . . the general idea would provide the option for individual development, the conditions for equality of opportunity and dignity of existence, and the provision of minimal choice making power for all persons.

Today, and in the near future, there are and will be programs which approximate or support the evolution of a guaranteed income. If the optimal goals of free choice resources are kept in mind, these programs can be positive and useful transitional vehicles.

The first and most tenuous of these vehicles are the existing state and Federal loan programs. Although these programs have little influence upon elementary and secondary educational alternatives, they provide a means of temporarily expanding a person's growth and educational alternatives. Unfortunately, these same loans have the ultimate adverse effect of reducing a person's choice at later points in his life by sometimes weighty repayment obligations. One approach to the removal or reduction of these choice making constraints is the constant liberalization of cancellation and postponement options. Such a liberalization process might help to reduce the transitional frictions that will undoubtedly occur with the evolution of guaranteed income.

A second group of vehicles approaching a guaranteed income

takes the form of grants, scholarships, and the currently proposed voucher system. There are two drawbacks to these vehicles. One is that their quantity is extremely limited. Another is that they provide some new educational alternatives but actually severely limit the number of choices supported under their auspices.

As the concept of growth and education expands beyond the boundaries of a formal educational "system" or "school" as well as the limitations traditionally ascribed by age, the above two forms of monetary choice supporting resources will become increasingly inferior to the general concept of a guaranteed income. Loans have the long-run effect of reducing certain choice options while the various forms of grants are limited in availability and scope. Guaranteed income would, on the other hand, allow individuals to design and choose their own educational objectives and systems without the constraints of existing systems and expectations as well as provide each person with choice and renewal opportunities throughout his life without curtailing his growth at a later date. . . .

CONCLUSION

Both society and its educational institutions are amidst a major transition period. Both face the need to adjust to fundamentally new premises if they are to survive this transition and still retain a humanistic outlook. On one hand, we are faced with a growing necessity for more communication and sharing of responsibility by all social segments. On the other hand, we face the prospects of historically unparalleled affluence and freedom.

Although we have not reached a utopian situation and it will be a long time before we even approach one, man's situation has more potential than ever before. In many senses, we are approaching a state which will allow man rather than the forces around him to determine his own nature and fate. Both the promises and responsibilities of this situation are frightening. Essentially, it means that we must place increasing faith upon the individual to determine and enact his own development, as well as responsibility to nature and society.

Throughout history man has had to exert numerous controls and constraints upon himself. This is still true but to a different and lesser degree. The reasons and fears behind many of these constraints are disappearing and changing. Man no longer needs nor is desirous of tolerating the continuance of many of these constraints. The transition we face demands the expansion of individual human freedom and responsibility through self-discipline.

In their own way, people are changing. They are becoming more individualized, more themselves, more human. Educational and other institutions must adjust to meet and facilitate this change.

Section E

the work-income link: toward post-economic motivation

Throughout the bulk of history human livelihood has been directly linked to the performance of work. Generation after generation was taught "If one did not work, one did not eat." Today, however, that link is becoming increasingly indirect. Although only small portions of our work-age population are affected, signs point to a gradual weakening of the iron law that demands continual work effort as the price for survival. Indeed, several complimentary forces are moving us toward a general collapse of the work-income link as we now know it. Let's look at some of the indications. First, the extension of years spent on education has divorced more and more people from the traditional work-income link. Second, the growing complexities of advanced industrial economies are likewise disrupting this link. Economic cycles, shifting market demands, job obsolescence, technological displacement, and the growing tendency toward temporary or project work assignments have fostered long and more frequent transitions between work periods. Third, the exploding productive capacities of our abundance regions coupled with the necessity for balancing supply and demand have created the need for a vast, accelerating expansion of credit, allowing the expenditure of income not yet received through work activities. Finally, the increasing commitment within affluent societies to assist the needy through various forms of welfare is further cutting the relationship between work and income.

In the most general sense the growing dissolution of the work-income link is the result of a two-edged sword. On the one hand, the growing complexities of advanced industrial societies have bred casualties such as cyclical unemployment and changing skill requirements. On the other hand, today's affluence has fostered a more compassionate and supportive response to disjunctures in income than was possible under the harsh conditions of scarcity that dominated the not-so-distant past. These conditions have led to a multitude of private and government-sponsored income-maintenance and education programs designed to ease the burden of those who for one reason or another are unable to secure their livelihood directly from work activities. In the field of education we have provided student loans, scholarships, and programs which seek to integrate work and education. Readjustment and transitional problems have been met with unemployment insurance, severance pay, and drawing in advance on social security and pension plans. General credit has been expanded through the use of credit cards, overdraw privileges for checking accounts, and vastly liberalized loan contracts. Finally, for the less fortunate, welfare has been developed in the form of cash allowances, food stamps, and limited medical aid programs.

Existing income-maintenance programs do reduce the problems associated with faltering links between work and income, but regrettably, they are often suboptimal and frequently woefully inadequate in terms of their stated purposes. For instance, scholarships are extremely limited, and loans provide no adjustment mechanisms for faulty educational planning like that which led to the teacher and engineer gluts of the 1970s. Readjustment and transitional income programs do not cover all workers, provide too little aid, and are frequently terminated too soon. Credit is too often reserved for those who do not truly need it, and interest rates are in many cases exploitive. Welfare programs are riddled with inconsistencies, incur massive administrative expenses, demean the self-respect of participants, and generally provide inadequate and inequitable assistance. And in addition, our current array of income-maintenance programs is swiftly proving to be too complex to be understood by the average citizen, and too cumbersome to be efficiently and responsibly administered.

During the last few years the increasingly apparent inadequacies of our income-maintenance programs have inspired proposals for a general guaranteed income plan, which would insure all persons of a minimum income floor as a basic human right. Such a program would cause fundamental changes in the motivations, goals, and organization of work. In this section we have chosen two selections to explain the general concept of guaranteed income, evaluate its likelihood, and speculate about its ramifications. First, Nobel-prize-winning economist Paul Samuelson explains the basic concept of guaranteed income and predicts its inevitability. Then, futurist Robert Theobald describes the long-run necessity and consequences of guaranteed income.

guaranteed income today:
an idea whose time has come

Paul Samuelson

WELFARE ASSISTANCE

In every county and city there exists some apparatus for help to the destitute. These programs involve some element of direct aid at the same time that they often involve some element of transfer of abstract purchasing power. Thus in a Northern city a welfare mother with three young children may be receiving a check of $300 per month. Some of this she may be free to spend as she wishes; but some part of it will be under the close supervision of the welfare worker assigned to her case, who lays down guidelines of how much can go for clothing, house furnishings, and so forth.

Because the minimum standards insisted upon by modern society have risen significantly, the cost of welfare programs has burgeoned in recent decades. Consequently there is great unease among the tax-paying citizenry over such programs. Thus a Gallup-like poll in 1970 would show that half the public think that welfare assistance is shot through with gross abuses. Anecdotes are told of mothers who spend hundreds of dollars fixing their teeth or buying color television sets with funds that ought to go for vitamin A drops for the baby. Illegitimate births among mothers on relief are not greeted with the same tolerance as are similar blessed events among starlets and the jet set.

Among informed professionals in the area of welfare and social psychology, there is a similar feeling of disquiet with the present apparatus of welfare assistance. It is indeed costly. And often inefficient. It puts a heavy psychological tax upon the recipients, and in some cases helps to create a caste of poor who must be taken care of in the same way that their parents were taken care of. A higher standard of sexual and other conduct is often demanded of those on relief than the critics themselves can, with all their advantages, live up to. Thus, in some states the father of a family on relief may find that the noblest thing he can do to enhance the well-being of his loved ones is to leave home and disappear. Only then can his wife and children continue to get the aid they desperately need. (And lest he should return at night, the social-service caseworker is often supposed to initiate surprise bed checks—a practice that strikes sensitive observers as despicable.) [1]

. . . If a relief father were to be offered a job that paid him several hundred dollars, taking that job might in many states cost him several thousand dollars in the form of lost relief payments. Even a steady job at a minimum wage of $1.60 per hour might represent a net loss to him in terms of what is left over after *deductions* from his relief allotments.

Economically, the traditional system of welfare payments geared to need and earnings involves massive hidden costs in terms of *disincentive* effects. Literally billions of dollars of lost gross national product result from the disincentive structure of existing relief systems.

THE NEGATIVE INCOME TAX

Contemplating the great economic inefficiency of existing welfare programs to mitigate poverty and inequality, economists of quite varied political persuasions have come to agreement on the need for a basic reform in the modern welfare state. A New Frontiersman like James Tobin of Yale and a Goldwater and Nixon adviser like Milton Friedman agree that it will be both cheaper and more humane to replace or supplement the mess that we call welfare assistance by a federal program that utilizes the efficient apparatus of the tax structure to attune incomes with needs.

Here is an idea whose time has come. Most economists have for some time favored it. Even President Nixon, in one of his early 1969 decisions, was persuaded to recommend to Congress a family-allow-

---

[1] A changing list of programs, and names for programs, characterize the battle against poverty. Before his 1963 assassination, John Kennedy decided to initiate a special program for Appalachia, to alleviate rural and miners' poverty. Under Lyndon Johnson, the Office of Economic Opportunity (OEO) was set up, and manpower and labor market programs (the Job Corps, etc.) and Vista and Head Start programs were initiated. Under Nixon, these have been reshaped and coordinated with his proposed family-allowance plan.

ance program which embodied much of the philosophy and mechanisms of the negative income tax. Indeed, almost everything is good about the negative income tax except its name—which sounds so negative. So call it, if you like, the "incentive-guaranteed-income" plan.

. . . The basic notion is simple. When I make $10,000 a year, I pay positive income taxes. . . . When I earn an extra thousand dollars, I do pay extra taxes, but only in fractional amounts so that I am strongly motivated to earn more in order to have more.

Now consider a family below some defined poverty level—say, $4,000, in a typical year in the early 1970s, for a couple with two children. Below that level they are deemed to have no capacity to pay any taxes; and indeed under current philosophies of equity and ability to pay, our democracy feels that they should receive government aids. In short, these aids constitute a tax in reverse—a *negative* income tax.

But here is where incentives come in. It is a common mistake to think that only the unemployed are poor, or that only fatherless families are poor. Statistics show that much of poverty is among the *working* poor—people who simply cannot earn in the marketplace what is today considered a minimum-needed income. They, and their children, are deemed to merit government help.

Yet how can these aids be given them so as not to deter their efforts and incentives? Here is where the negative income tax provides a great improvement over those welfare programs which deprive people of all assistance the moment they get even a poor job. (And, of course, those on assistance know this very well and are thus deterred from trying to improve their position.) Just as the positive income tax is geared between $10,000 and $11,000 to leave people with an incentive to better themselves, the formula for the negative income tax is gauged to leave the poor with more income after they have used their own efforts to raise their private earnings by a thousand dollars, or even by a dollar. Even when their total tax is negative, their marginal tax rate is always a positive fraction less than unity.

. . . Table 1 illustrates how a typical negative income tax might work. What is shown there for a family with two children could be easily modified in the case of more or fewer family members. And of course, as the country grows richer and can afford to be more generous, the formula could be changed to begin at a higher level and to define a poverty level that is higher both in dollar terms and perhaps in terms of dollars of constant purchasing power.

POSSIBLE FORMULA FOR NEGATIVE INCOME TAX

Private Earnings	Algebraic Tax (+ if tax; - if aid received)	After-Tax Income
$ 0	−$2,000	$2,000
1,000	− 1,500	2,500
2,000	− 1,000	3,000
3,000	− 500	3,500
4,000	0	4,000
5,000	+500	4,500

Table 1   Here, a couple with two children is guaranteed at least $2,000 a year, but is left with incentive to work. (Verify this in last column.) The poverty line . . . could be raised as the nation gets wealthier, and, of course, the formula can be modified for families of varying sizes. (adapted from Samuelson, *Economics*, 8th ed.)

The paramount advantages of the negative income tax are many.

1. It can replace much of present welfare assistance that destroys incentives.
2. It can help to equalize minimum levels of well-being over all the diverse regions of the United States.
3. It is less demeaning to the poor.
4. It could have various advantages of simple administration by the *Revenue Service*.[2]

[2] For more on the negative income tax, see the readings by James Tobin and Robert J. Lampman in P. A. Samuelson, *Readings [in Economics]* and the article by Milton Friedman in Melvin Laird, ed., *The Republican Papers* (Anchor Books, Doubleday & Company, Inc., Garden City, N.Y., 1969).

Chapter 13

guaranteed income tomorrow:

toward post-economic

motivation

Robert Theobald

. . . In mid-1965, it was still necessary to show that the idea of a
guaranteed income was a relevant one which was gaining serious
attention in the United States. In September 1966, some fifteen
months later, the guaranteed income is widely recognized as a short-
run possibility: the list of governmental organizations—the National
Commission on Technology, Automation and Economic Progress,
the White House Conference on Civil Rights, the Council of Economic Advisers, the Office of Economic Opportunity—which have
proposed its study is convincing evidence of the political resonance
of the concept. In Canada, prospects for the introduction of the
guaranteed income are even more advanced; it is under immediate
consideration for all those over sixty-five with subsequent extension
to the whole population being considered for the near future.

This evolution has continued during the last two years. Thus
an idea that was first rejected by almost all commentators as too
extreme to be worthy of practical consideration is today being rejected by many of those who are most convinced of the need for a
new socioeconomic order on the grounds that it promises no fundamental change in the present socioeconomy.

What brought about this dramatic shift in opinions? Certainly
the most striking factor has been the acceptance of direct payments
to the poor by Professor Milton Friedman, Senator Goldwater's economic adviser in the 1964 campaign. It has been increasingly argued
that if Milton Friedman is in favor of the measure, all those concerned with the welfare of the individual should automatically re-

ject the idea. Such "ad hominem" arguments should, of course, have no place in the debate on this subject.

It is therefore essential that the areas of agreement and disagreement among those supporting direct payments to the poor should be sharply differentiated. The first area of agreement is that the initial step on the way to eliminate poverty is to supply money rather than moral uplift, cultural refinements, extended education, retraining programs or makework jobs. In addition, it is agreed that the prime criterion for the distribution of funds should be the poverty of the individual rather than whether Congress is willing to pass special legislation supporting him: it is agreed, as a corollary, that many programs, such as those in agriculture, which were originally designed to help the poor, have become methods of subsidizing the rich. There is another area of agreement which is crucial. It is seen as vital that funds should be provided as an absolute right— that the size of grants should be determined on the basis of objective criteria rather than on the whims and prejudices of the bureaucrat. An absolute guarantee of payment should be incorporated in the legislation setting up direct payments to the poor.

It should be noted at this point that certain people have tried to undermine this last key element of the guaranteed income proposal. They have stated that we should introduce the idea of direct payments to the poor but that the availability of payments should be based on a bureaucratic determination of the eligibility of the individual for such payments. Such an elimination of the guarantee destroys the crucial element in the proposal and would threaten ever greater intervention in the personal life of the individual.

The recognition of the need to provide *guaranteed direct* payments to the poor on the basis of their *existing income levels* must necessarily be shared by all the proponents of a guaranteed income. Their motivations for suggesting such a scheme may, however, be very different; this can be most clearly seen by contrasting the approach of Milton Friedman with my own. Professor Friedman sees the fundamental economic problem as resulting from increasing government intervention in the economic system. He finds this development deeply disturbing for he believes that the economic system can be expected to work efficiently only if each individual is free to seek his own economic advantage. Perceiving as he does that much of the increase in government intervention in the economy results from the fact that it is impossible for the rulers of a modern state to allow any group of citizens to starve, Professor Friedman believes that we should devise measures that would ensure a minimum income for all and thus eliminate the major present cause of government intervention in the economy. It is essential, in his view, that the level of income not be set so high that it would detract from the incentive to work—while he has not proposed a precise level for grants, his illustrations have been couched in terms of an income floor of $1600 for a family of four.

Professor Friedman hopes that once such an allowance is available, society would not only cease to demand the introduction of further measures of government intervention but would acquiesce in the dismantling of the vast majority of the measures already in existence that were passed to help those less able to help themselves. He anticipates that as government measures are rescinded, and what he sees as the barriers to "self-help" are removed, the country would benefit from an access of the drives that made the ninetenth century so successful. The proposal of Professor Friedman can therefore be explained by his belief that we should re-create the conditions in which the individual can strive to maximize his economic satisfaction with the greatest degree of freedom and the minimum outside intervention.

While I agree with Professor Friedman that one of the main threats to the survival of freedom is the rapidly growing intervention of government bureaucracies in individual lives, my object in providing the individual with a guaranteed income is not to move back to unrestricted economic competition but rather to move forward into a new societal order. In my view, therefore, the guaranteed income must provide a standard of living adequate for decency—I believe that we should start with a minimum income of $3400 [1966 dollars] for a family of four. In addition, we must accept the certainty of a number of other changes in the distribution of resources —the first of these will be measures to protect those in the middle-income groups who lose their jobs as a consequence of cybernation.

For me, therefore, the guaranteed income represents the possibility of putting into effect the fundamental philosophic belief, which has recurred consistently in human history, that each individual has a right to a minimal share in the production of his society. The perennial shortage of almost all the necessities of life prevented the application of this belief until recent years: the coming of relative abundance in the rich countries gives man the power to achieve the goal of providing a minimum standard of living for all.

It is not enough, however, to state that it is *possible* for the society to provide a minimal standard of living for all. One should rather state that it is *essential* to do so. The present late-industrial age is burdened with problems arising from a mismatch between the needs of the human society and the pressures exerted by an economic production, distribution and consumption system so complex and interrelated as to need the whole of the national culture to be organized around it. While we allow this process to continue, the economic system will increasingly become a parasite on the total environment, depriving the men who create it of their psychological and social sustenance and, in return, providing them with only economic gains.

Recent developments have confirmed the theoretical judgment of Professor Charles Killingsworth of Michigan State University that even when the government is successful in balancing potential demand with available supply, if will still be impossible to employ all those with low skills and inadequate education. This view has so far been rejected by the Administration and most economists on the ground that the pace of improvement in educational accomplishments will counterbalance the increase in the efficiency of machines, and that special education and retraining programs will be adequate to deal with the relatively few people who require further help.

The August 1966 data on the labor force show clearly that even substantial movements toward full employment are no longer effective in drawing all of the labor force into employment and that it is the disadvantaged who suffer most severely. While over-all unemployment dropped from 4.6 per cent in the May–August 1965 period to 4.0 per cent in the May–August 1966 period, the unemployment rates for unskilled nonfarm workers dropped only from 7.8 to 7.6 per cent while the unemployment rate for Negro teenagers remained constant at 27 per cent.

The available statistics understate the social crisis that is now upon us, for many other workers theoretically "at work" in "jobs" perform little activity and none that gives meaning to their lives. Others still cling to the self-respect and societal esteem attached to their middle-income "skilled" or "management" job, but know that a machine-system or computer will shortly be ready to replace them. New tasks and new more complex processes that would never be accomplished by man are being assigned to the new, manless technology. In many areas man, the master, is less than technology, his servant. Conversely, we are witnessing a downgrading of human creativity as compared with the innovative potential of machine systems. Somehow, in any given area where man and machine compete, the output of the computer is more "authoritative," more "correct" than man's. So man's role is rapidly becoming that of obedient consumer, prompt obeyer of punch-card demands, apathetic observer of environmental abuse and human degradation, of water pollution, lethal air, the continuing waste of natural resources, the aimless misery of the unemployed and the underpaid, the neurotic defense mechanisms of the occupationally threatened middle class.

Man's structuring into the economic necessities of the present age cannot be reversed without the guaranteed income, which aims to provide rights to resources adequate for the dignified life. Today's socioeconomic system uses a very simple mechanism for distributing resources: it assumes that the overwhelming proportion of those seeking jobs can find them and that the incomes received will allow the job holder to live in dignity. Such a distribution mechanism requires that enough effective demand exist to take up all the goods and services that can be produced by all the capital and labor that can be effectively used.

John Maynard Keynes has shown why this chain *must* be preserved if the industrial socioeconomy is to function, and economists have therefore come to concentrate on the necessity of balancing supply and demand and thus ensuring the availability of sufficient jobs. This has been generally acceptable because it has been believed that more consumption led to higher standards of living; that "enough" is $1000 more than present income. Recent experimentation, however, has confirmed the significance of the problem of sensory overload; that is, of an inability to absorb more than a certain amount of experience in a given time. This can be illustrated on one level by the new anesthesia technique, used particularly in dentistry, of providing the patient with earphones and then raising the level of sound to the point at which pain ceases to be felt. A similar phenomenon occurs during world tours: it becomes impossible to absorb more sights and sounds. The implications of this understanding of sensory overload are critical because there is increasingly general agreement that creativity depends upon a period of low sensory activity; in other words, upon an opportunity to reflect. As individuals come to realize the reality of sensory overload, they can be expected voluntarily to restrict their input of sensory perceptions; this will inevitably force limits on purchases and on travel.

In addition, society will be forced to limit waste by changing its patterns of rewards and sanctions. Arguments on this subject cannot be based, in my opinion, on an assumed shortage of raw materials, for man's ability to produce new materials through physics and chemistry could grow at least as fast as his need for materials. Rather the need for limiting waste—whether caused by exaggerated rates of obsolescence, the development of a throwaway culture, the acceptance of polluting by-products or other reasons—will be based on our growing knowledge of ecology; on the necessity to limit the degree of change in the environment if man is to survive.

The guaranteed income is therefore essential for both short-run and long-run reasons. In the short-run, it is required because an ever-growing number of people—blue-collar, white-collar, middle-management and professional—cannot compete with machines; in the absence of the guaranteed income the number of people in hopeless, extreme poverty will increase. In the long run, we will require a justification for the distribution of resources that is not based on job-holding, because this is the only way we can break the present necessity to ensure that supply and demand remain in balance: a necessity that we have just seen is incompatible with continued development of the individual and continued survival of the world.

Both of these justifications are commonly attacked on the grounds that any adequate guaranteed-income scheme would limit incentives. However, the historical and anthropological record makes it clear that economic motivation is not the only way to get people to work—indeed there is considerable evidence that it is not necessarily the most effective way. The inevitable increase in wealth over the next decades will itself largely destroy the financial incentive—if average family income (in 1966 prices) is of the order of $28,000 by the year 2000 as seems probable, most people will be motivated less by the possibility of increasing their income and more by other potentials. Indeed, this pattern is already emerging in the upper-income brackets, particularly among the young.

It is perhaps appropriate to conclude this essay by explaining the reasons for the rapid acceptance of the guaranteed income and the implications of this acceptance for patterns of further discussion. Conrad Arensberg pointed out . . . that the guaranteed-income proposal has the two aspects that are necessary for a successful innovation. "The first effect of a successfully adaptive . . . innovation of any kind is to hold onto something tried and true, to conserve the old in the face of change. In paleontology this conservative first effect of evolutionary advance is called Romer's rule; it could well be called that in cultural and social advance, too. When the proposed guaranteed income works to preserve and restore the free market, to leave unchanged private property, to holster and to restore freedom to choose one's own work, buy and sell at will, in short, to advance by combining old and new, it is on the right, the tested evolutionary track. The second effect of a successfully adaptive innovation of any kind, biological or social, is quite other than conservative; indeed, it is the opening of a vast new door, a splendid serendipity."

. . . This, of course, will be feasible only if we become willing to recognize that all significant actions will *necessarily* have both favorable and unfavorable consequences: the problem is to choose the course of action that will minimize unfavorable effects and maximize favorable possibilities. It is for this reason that we can no longer accept the patterns of the past where supporters of a proposed course of action pointed only to the favorable results and its opponents discussed only the unfavorable impacts. It is my conviction on this point that . . . the guaranteed income would indeed have unfavorable as well as favorable consequences—it was therefore depressing to find that many reviewers were prepared to dismiss [*The Guaranteed Income*] on the grounds that it did not promise "Instant Utopia."

It is vital that we develop new methods of discussion, debate and dialogue that will allow us to develop the fullest possible understanding of the results of proposed actions. It is in this context that the difference between Professor Friedman and myself gains its crucial importance. The attitude of Professor Friedman emphasizes the need to study the type of tax system that could be used to introduce direct payments to the poor but leads one essentially to ignore the long-run potentials of such a step for the socioeconomy. This consequence is inevitable, for Professor Friedman has assumed that the guaranteed income is being introduced to preserve, and strengthen, the industrial-age socioeconomy—it therefore appears irrelevant to examine what changes the guaranteed income would cause.

I believe that we will be able to gain sufficient understanding of the implications of the guaranteed income and the other changes now occurring in society only if a far wider spectrum of people are challenged to participate in the task of inventing the future. . . .

some alternative
futures for work

In 1936 C. C. Furnas published *The Next Hundred Years,* which was long regarded as a brilliant speculation of future events and conditions. Today, however, we recognize its numerous shortcomings: space travel was overlooked, and the worldwide ramifications of nuclear power and the atomic bomb were not foreseen. This excellent futuristic study does, however, provide an illustration of how even the most painstaking speculations are subject to unforeseen variables. The point is that every view of the future we currently envision could be radically altered by an unexpected breakthrough, say, instantaneous matter transmission.

While the variables of our evolving world are complex, the need for and plausibility of speculating about the future still exists. Because of this need, the discipline of futuristics has become increasingly more methodological and sophisticated. Iron-clad prophecies are not only considered unwise but, for the most part, foolish; instead rather flexible speculations are made, subject to the behavior of a number of variables. In many cases single overall predictions are avoided in favor of several alternative models of future conditions, which conceptualize possible choices and recognize the human potential to alter or influence our future, once the alternatives become evident.

As our ability to predict the future becomes more sophisticated, we are becoming increasingly aware that the future is unlikely to develop into a central or universally common format. Rather, most indications suggest that it will bring a constantly increasing diversity.[1] In a very general sense, this trend toward diversity reflects a basic ecological principle. Observations of all forms of life reveal that successful biological species tend to become more heterogeneous in order to expand their versatility for survival and growth.[2]

As expanding options permit human priorities to shift more and more toward concerns about finding personal identity, pursuing dreams and ideals, and exploring new experiences, we can expect a burgeoning of diversity in all aspects of life. Most of us will make efforts to match the goals and actions of our lives to our specific mental and physical natures—to become more individualized. One important effect of the tendency toward more individualization will be increasingly varied concepts of work. From this perspective, it is impossible to put forth an overall vision of the future of work; we can, however, provide descriptions of some alternative likelihoods, differing greatly but related by their common treatment of work as a goal-oriented human activity. The differences arise from the conditions that people of the future may accept and the goals they may pursue to satisfy their sense of values and productivity.

The first selection here, by futurists Herman Kahn and Anthony Wiener, examines some of the general issues concerning work; it assumes that economic affluence will keep growing at the existing rate. Regarded as "surprise-free" projections, the possibilities Kahn and Wiener perceive actually suggest major changes in our concept of work, even for those seeking more of what we now produce. Next, French technologist Jacques Ellul conjures up a vision of humans becoming "cogs" in nonorganic productive machinery because of an overdependence on technology. Then, Ernest Callenbach draws upon the philosophies and life-styles of the counter-culture to develop a view of human productivity that rejects excessive materialism and seeks to move toward self-sufficiency and intrinsically motivated production and consumption. Finally, Carolyn Symonds offers a speculation on the "best of all possible worlds," in which advanced technology is used for human purposes and life and work are integrated into a productive, self-fulfilling abundance.

[1] Alvin Toffler presents an excellent discussion of future diversity in *Future Shock* (New York: Random House, 1970), pp. 223–77.

[2] Eugene P. Odum, *Ecology* (New York: Holt, Rinehart & Winston, Inc., 1963), pp. 85–86.

Chapter 14

the future meanings of work:
some "surprise-free"
observations

Herman Kahn and Anthony Wiener

. . . We construct a hypothetical pattern of events in quantitative terms—that is, in terms of measures of productivity, population, growth, work, leisure, and affluence—for the Standard World and its variations. We assume a continuing production of various new technologies of the kind we discussed in the previous chapters. It is difficult to estimate the impact of such technological changes on the average productivity of the labor force. One can, of course, estimate specific increases in productivity by examining applications of innovations in specific industries, but these studies tend to underestimate the total impact—in part because one simply does not know how widely and ingeniously the new techniques may be used. Nor can one predict how efficient the new technique will be after the initial learning period has been exploited. Most important of all, it is almost impossible to form any good estimate of synergistic, let alone serendipitous, effects.

Therefore . . . we shall simply postulate that recent rates in such things as increase in productivity will at least be equaled or increased in the future—at least over the long run. More specifically, we shall write a moderately optimistic economic scenario of how things may go, if there are no major wars or depressions, for the next thirty-three years or so.

What is meant by "optimistic" is illustrated by the following graph of GNP per capita. . . . Table 1 summarizes for ten major countries the GNP per capita growth rate, first along the longest available trend and second as we assume more likely for the next thirty-three years.

"The Future Meanings of Work: Some 'Surprise-Free' Observations" (editor's title). Excerpted from Herman Kahn and Anthony Wiener, *The Year 2000* (New York: The Macmillan Company, 1967), pp. 118–19, 122, 123, 186–89, 193, 194, 198–202, and 208–11. Copyright © 1967 by The Hudson Institute, Inc. Reprinted with permission of The Macmillan Company.

Table 1   COMPARATIVE FORECASTS OF GNP PER CAPITA TO YEAR 2000.- TEN MAJOR COUNTRIES

	1965 GNP/CAP. 1965 U.S. $	Medium Forecast Growth Rate % Per Year	Medium Forecast Year 2000 GNP/CAP. 1965 U.S. $	Forecast Using More Long-term Trend Growth Rate % Per Year	Forecast Using More Long-term Trend Year 2000 GNP/CAP. 1965 U.S. $	Earliest Data For Long-term Trend
U.S.	3557	3.0	10160	1.8	6750	1869-73
Canada	2464	3.1	7070	1.6	4300	1870-79
France	1964	3.7	6830	1.6	3400	1810-20
W. Germany	1905	4.1	7790	1.8	3600	1860-69'
U.K.	1804	3.7	6530	1.5	3000	1860-69|
U.S.S.R.	1288	3.7	4650	2.8	3400	1870
Italy	1101	4.1	4450	2.4	2500	1862-68
Japan	857	6.8	8590	3.7	3100	1878-87
India	99	2.9	270	2.1	205	1950
China	98	3.5	321	3.1	285	1933
Unweighted average		4.1		2.3		

Sources: Growth rates: computed from GNP per capita 1965 and present medium forecast to 2000 as given in Table XIV [in *The Year 2000*]. Forecasts using long-term trends based on studies of sources reported in Mark Wehle's memorandum, HI-846-RR.

One reason for using growth rates higher than those indicated by the long-term trend is that they fit well with the recent experience of most countries. What is now the comparatively short-term trend may be the future long-term trend. . . .

These considerations apply to both the developed and less-developed countries. . . .

THE POSTINDUSTRIAL SOCIETY

[The items listed in Table 2] seem to us likely to be characteristic of the emerging situation, especially in the United States. . . .

We shall discuss most of these issues by simply mentioning them, or occasionally conjecturing very briefly on their significance, without attempting to be systematic or exhaustive. Many of the statements will nonetheless be in conclusionary form, mainly because it is easier to focus or provoke discussion in a short paragraph if one states a position than if one attempts to give several alterna-

Table 2   THE POSTINDUSTRIAL (OR POST-MASS CONSUMP-
TION) SOCIETY
1. Per capita income about fifty times the preindustrial
2. Most "economic" activities are tertiary and quaternary (ser-
   vice-oriented) rather than primary or secondary (production-
   oriented)
3. Business firms no longer the major source of innovation
4. There may be more "consentives" (vs. "marketives")
5. Effective floor on income and welfare
6. "Efficiency" no longer primary
7. Market plays diminished role compared to public sector and
   "social accounts"
8. Widespread "cybernation"
9. "Small world"
10. Typical "doubling time" between three and thirty years
11. Learning society
12. Rapid improvement in educational institutions and techniques
13. Erosion (in middle class) of work-oriented, achievement-
    oriented, advancement-oriented values
14. Erosion of "national interest" values?
15. Sensate, secular, humanist, perhaps self-indulgent criteria
    become central

[1]See Footnote 9 in Chapter 1. [The Year 2000].

tives in truncated form. In all cases we tend to "believe in" the position indicated, though perhaps tentatively. These conjectures are
no more than our current working hypotheses and are clearly more
controversial than most aspects of our Standard World.

It may be useful to compare the shift away from primary and
secondary occupations to an earlier transition made in the United
States in the mid-nineteenth century. In that predominantly agricultural society, 55 per cent of the labor force were farmers, while
today only about 5 per cent of the labor force is engaged in agriculture. . . .

A similar transformation, though not so extreme, may develop
with respect to business activities in a postindustrial society. A
smaller percentage of people may be engaged in business, and the
very success of private business may make its further successes seem
less exciting and dramatic. While businessmen will probably continue to be deeply occupied with their affairs, the issues of finance,
investment, production, sales, and distribution that have so long
been dominant concerns of so many Americans and Europeans will
very likely dwindle in interest. American industry has already been
concerned about its declining attractiveness for college graduates,

especially for the most intellectually gifted segments of the group, and there may eventually be a general lowering of business morale.

The postindustrial era is likely to be more of a "learning society" than today's. In part this is because of the "information explosion," but mostly because of the rapidity of change. . . . The computers of 1967 have about ten times the performance capacity of those of 1964 and 1965, which means that concepts of appropriate computer functions that were perfectly valid for the computers of two or three years ago must be reviewed and sometimes completely changed. In many cases the new concepts that must be devised in order to deal adequately with today's potentialities are very different from those of two or three years ago.

While the computer is a fairly extreme example of rapid change, it is reasonably indicative—though the more likely time for significant change in most areas would be closer to ten or twenty than two or three years. Thus, if the annual per capita increase in income is 4 per cent, then per capita income will double every eighteen years. Such a doubling is clearly a most significant event. Or to take another example, television, which was almost unheard of in private homes in 1946 and 1947, had by 1955 changed American living patterns in a very marked way. In this case, the exact significance of the changes is yet unevaluated. (For example, it is difficult to be sure whether or not it makes a great difference, or how, that large numbers of children and their parents spend an average of several hours every day passively watching a flickering screen.) To give another example, it takes about twenty to fifty years for most countries to double their populations, so there may easily be two or three doublings within one lifetime. Similarly, a country may, within one lifetime, change from being largely or overwhelmingly rural to largely or overwhelmingly urban. Or the number of kilowatts generated per year, the passenger miles in autos or planes, numbers of telephones, and so on may increase by factors of five to a hundred in a decade or two. Any of these changes occurring by themselves could be important. If all of them, and others as well, occur more or less simultaneously, the total rate of change and the need for large adaptions become fantastic. The term future shock has been used to describe the corresponding "acculturation" trauma. These changes seem likely to increase in number, kind, and rate at least for the next three or four decades. The corresponding need for adjustment, adaptation, and control is likely to be one of the most characteristic and central phenomena of the early postindustrial era, although there is some possibility that it will not be either as pervasive or dramatic in a later time period, simply because there may be a deliberate slowing down in order to "take it easier" and to avoid or meliorate consequences of change. . . .

ALIENATION AMIDST AFFLUENCE

. . . We are attempting to describe a plausible and culturally consistent projection of a culture, values, and style of life consistent with other features of our Standard World of the year 2000. . . . We can take what we now know about past and current American styles of life together with some current trends . . . and on this basis try to assess the consequences of some simple, basic trends. . . . These include relatively easy affluence, new technology, absence of absorbing international challenges, and considerable but not disastrous population growth. We must ask, in effect, how these trends might furnish or constrain possibilities for change. . . .

[Postindustrial Affluence and Work]

[One] . . . salient factor seems likely to be a vastly increased availability of goods and such services as transportation and communication. A second is a likely increase in leisure and a concomitant reduction of the pressures of work. A third is the likelihood of important technological changes in such areas as psychopharmacology, with possible radical consequences for culture and styles of life. Perhaps the most important is a likely absence of stark "life and death" economic and national security issues.

How can we assess the impact of these changes even on a current situation which itself is imperfectly understood? One of the greatest problems of all psychological and sociological speculation has to do with the dialectical quality of the processes involved. It is difficult to know whether to extrapolate trends or to postulate reactions against the same trends. For example, if work will occupy fewer hours of the average person's life, it is plausible to speculate that for this reason work will become less important. On the other hand, it is at least equally plausible that the change in the role of work may cause work as an issue to come to new prominence. The values surrounding work, which in the developed areas have evolved over centuries, may emerge into a new flux and once again become controversial sources of problems within a society and for many individuals. The ideologies that surround work and give it justification and value, in individual and social terms, may become strength-ened in support of what remains of work; on the other hand, they may increasingly come into doubt and become the objects of reaction and rebellion. Indeed both trends may materialize simultaneously in different parts of society and may cause conflicts within many individuals. Clearly one can write many scenarios here, with many different branching points. These quandaries must be resolved ultimately by at least partly intuitive and subjective judgments; the most one can claim for such speculations is that no alternative possibility seems much more likely. . . .

Success Breeds Failure: Affluence and the Collapse of Bourgeois Values

John Maynard Keynes addressed himself to this dilemma [of whether increased leisure can be consistent with continued economic growth] in one of the earliest and still one of the best short discussions of some of the issues raised by the accumulation of wealth through investment.[1] As he put it,

> . . . the economic problem, the struggle for subsistence, always has been hitherto the primary, most pressing problem of the human race. If the economic problem is solved, mankind will be deprived of its traditional purpose.
>   Will this be of a benefit? If one believes at all in the real values of life, the prospect at least opens up the possibility of benefit. Yet I think with dread of the readjustment of the habits and instincts of the ordinary man, bred into him for countless generations, which he may be asked to discard within a few decades. . . . thus for the first time since his creation man will be faced with his real, his permanent problem—how to use his freedom from pressing economic cares, how to occupy his leisure, which science and compound interest will have won for him, to live wisely and agreeably and well.

There are those who would argue that with increased freedom from necessity men will be freed for more generous, public-spirited, and humane enterprises. It is a commonplace of the American consensus that it is poverty and ignorance that breed such evils as Communism, revolutions, bigotry, and race hatred. Yet we know better than to expect that the absence of poverty and ignorance will result in a triumph of virtue or even of the benign. On the contrary, it is equally plausible that a decrease in the constraints formerly imposed by harsher aspects of reality will result in large numbers of "spoiled

[1] "Economic Possibilities for our Grandchildren" (1930), reprinted in J. M. Keynes, *Essays in Persuasion* (New York: W. W. Norton, 1963), quoting from pp. 366–67.

children." At the minimum many may become uninterested in the administration and politics of a society that hands out "goodies" with unfailing and seemingly effortless regularity.

One may choose almost at will from among available hypotheses that may seem to apply to the situation, and one reaches contrary conclusions depending upon the choice that is made; this indeterminacy is perhaps a measure of the inadequacy of contemporary social thought as a basis for generalization, relative to the complexity of human phenomena.

For example, one may take the Dollard *et al.*[2] frustration-aggression hypothesis and conclude that aggressiveness will be greatly tranquilized in a society that provides much less external and realistic frustration. This is opposed to the more complex and more psychoanalytically oriented point of view of Freud who points to the role that frustrations imposed by external reality may play in shoring up the defenses of the character structure—defenses that are crucial strengths and that were acquired through learning, with difficulty, as an infant to defer gratification and to mediate among conflicting energies of instinctual impulses, conscience, and the opportunities and dangers of the real world.[3] Research might show, if research could be done on such a subject, that many an infantile and narcissistic personality has matured only when faced with the necessity of earning a living—others only when faced with the necessity for facing up to some personal challenge, such as military service or participation in family responsibility. (The well-known finding that suicide rates drop sharply during wars and economic depressions is subject to diverse interpretation, but it may suggest that such external challenges can serve crucial integrative or compensatory functions for some personalities, and perhaps, less dramatically, for many others.) This is not to say that equally effective or perhaps superior external challenges could not be found to substitute for the working role—or wartime experience—as a maturing or reality-focusing influence. If they are not found, however, while the economy and international and other threats make fewer demands, the de-

[2] John Dollard *et al.*, *Frustration and Aggression* (New Haven, Conn.: Yale University Press, 1939).

[3] As Freud pointed out, "Laying stress upon importance of work has a greater effect than any other technique of living in the direction of binding the individual more closely to reality; in his work he is at least securely attached to a part of reality, the human community . . . and yet . . . the great majority work only when forced by necessity, and this natural human aversion to work gives rise to the most difficult social problems." *Civilization and Its Discontents* (London: Hogarth Press, 1930), p. 34, note 1.

cline of the values of work and national service may have some destructive effect.

Thus there may be a great increase in selfishness, a great decline of interest in government and society as a whole, and a rise in
the more childish forms of individualism and in the more antisocial
forms of concern for self and perhaps immediate family. Thus, paradoxically, the technological, highly productive society, by demanding less of the individual, may decrease his economic frustrations but
increase his aggressions against the society. Certainly here would be
fertile soil for what has come to be known as alienation.

The word alienation has been used in many different senses,
some of them well defined and some in the context of systems of explanation and prescription for the ailment.[4] The young Karl Marx,
for example, followed Ludwig Feuerbach (and to some extent anticipated Freud's *Civilization and its Discontents*) in the belief that
alienation resulted from civilized man's "unnatural" repression of
his instinctual, especially sexual, nature. Later, however, Marx concluded that alienation resulted from the worker's relationship to
labor that had to be done for the profit of another; the cure was
to have the worker "own" the means of production; thus alienation
could be reduced by shortening the working day,[5] and "the worker
therefore feels himself at home only during his leisure." [6]

The alienation that we speculate may result from affluence
could have little or nothing to do with whether the society is capitalist or socialist. In either case the control of the decision-making
apparatus would be perceived as beyond the reach of and in fact of
little interest for the average person. Thus, whatever the economic
system, the politics (and even the culture) of plenty could become
one not of contentment but of cynicism, emotional distance, and
hostility. More and more the good life would be defined in Epicu-

---

[4] There is little doubt that this word has been used to refer to too many
different phenomena, and too many different hypotheses concerning the causal
relations among the phenomena. This is illustrated in the comprehensive but
diffuse collection of materials edited by Gerald Sykes, *Alienation, The Cultural
Climate of Our Time* (New York: George Braziller, 1964), 2 vols. For an interesting and critical historical survey, see Lewis Feuer, "What is Alienation? The Career of a Concept," in Stein and Vidich, eds., *Sociology on Trial,* (Englewood
Cliffs, N.J.: Prentice-Hall, Inc., 1965). Feuer argues against the term on the ground
that: "The career of this concept, from Calvin's depiction of man, the original
sinner, alienated from God for all time, to the modern notion of man alienated
somehow in every form of social organization, indicates indeed that its dominant
overtone is social defeat."

[5] *Capital,* vol. II.

[6] *Economic and Philosophical Manuscripts* (1844), p. 84.

rean or materialistic, rather than Stoic, or bourgeois terms. The enchantment of private values combined with the increased sense of futility about public values would also entail a kind of despair about the long-run future of the whole society. More and more people would act on the aphorism currently attributed to a leader of the new student left: "If you've booked passage on the Titanic, there's no reason to travel steerage."

Thus the classical American middle-class, work-oriented, advancement-oriented, achievement-oriented attitudes might be rejected for the following reasons:

1. Given an income per worker by the year 2000 of well over ten thousand dollars in today's dollars.[7] It may become comparatively easy for intelligent Americans to earn ten to twenty thousand dollars a year without investing very intense energies in their jobs—in effect they will be able to "coast" at that level.

2. It may become comparatively easy for an American to obtain several thousand dollars a year from friends and relatives or other sources, and to subsist without undergoing any real hardship, other than deprivation of luxuries. (Informal polls in the Cambridge, East Village, and Haight Ashbury areas indicate that many "hippies" get along on about ten dollars per week, as do many CORE and SNCC workers.)

3. Welfare services and public facilities will generally probably put a fairly high "floor" under living standards, even in terms of luxuries such as parks, beaches, museums, and so on.

4. With money plentiful, its subjective "marginal utility" would probably tend to diminish, and there would probably be a greatly increased emphasis on things that "money cannot buy."

5. Economic and social pressures to conform may diminish as the affluent society feels increasingly that it can "afford" many kinds of slackness and deviation from the virtues that were needed in earlier times to build an industrial society.

6. If the "Puritan ethic" becomes superfluous for the functioning of the economy, the conscience-dominated character type associated with it would also tend to disappear. Parents would no longer be strongly motivated to inculcate traits such as diligence, punctuality, willingness to postpone or forego satisfaction, and similar virtues no longer relevant to the socioeconomic realities in which children are growing up.

7. Yet the need to "justify" the new patterns may remain, and to the extent that there is any residual guilt about the abandonment of

[7] See projections of United States family incomes in Chap. III [*The Year 2000*].

the nineteenth- and early twentieth-century values, there would be exaggerated feelings *against* vocational success and achievement. Many intellectuals and contributors to popular culture would help to make the case against "bourgeois," "managerial," "bureaucratic," "industrial," "Puritanical," and "preaffluent" values. There would then be considerable cultural support for feelings ranging from indifference to outright contempt for any sort of success or achievement that has economic relevance.

Other factors would augment these effects. For example, presumably by the year 2000 much more will be known about mood-affecting drugs, and these drugs will probably be used by many as a means of escape from daily life. At the same time, the young, those without responsibility in the social system, will be increasingly alienated by a society that conspicuously fails to meet what it judges to be minimal standards of social justice and purpose (standards which look impossibly Utopian to decision-makers). Ideological movements would form to rationalize and justify rebellion and renunciation of old "obsolete" values by youth from all classes and strata of society. Less articulate but equally rebellious young people would contribute to a great rise in crime and delinquency. Other symptoms of social pathology, such as mental illness, neurosis, divorce, suicide, and the like would also probably increase. Traditional religious doctrines might either continue to lose force or continue to be reinterpreted, revised, and secularized so as to pose few obstacles to the current general way of life.

On the other hand, the resources of society for dealing with these problems, perhaps in a (suffocatingly?) paternalistic way, would also have been greatly augmented. Before discussing the differences that might be made by social responses to these problems, let us see how they might affect various social groups. . . .

CROSS-CULTURAL COMPARISONS

. . . In the previous six thousand years of recorded history civilized man, by and large, lived in societies not too dissimilar economically from that of Indonesia today, in which the average income was, give or take a factor or two, the equivalent of about one hundred dollars per capita. (Even the size of the larger societies, e.g., the Roman Empire or the Han Empire, was about the same in population as Indonesia today—about one hundred million people.)

The Industrial Revolution was, in many ways, a more important and more rapid change than any that had preceded. The changes that seem likely in the next thirty-three years also seem likely to lead to some results that are entirely unprecedented. Nevertheless we would suggest that some of the prospects for the year 2000 are, in effect, a return to a sort of new Augustinian age. Conditions (in the superdeveloped countries at least) could then differ from those of the early and mid-twentieth centuries—in some important ways—much as the early Roman Empire differed from the pre-classical world. We are all too familiar with clichés about the decline of the Roman Empire, but for the better part of the first two hundred years the Roman Empire enjoyed almost unparalleled good government, peace and prosperity. And it should be noted that it also began in an "age of anxiety" and apprehension. Arguments are often heard to the effect that the "moral fibre" of the Romans somehow "degenerated" because of a lack of challenge during the period of stability and prosperity. While the issues of cause and effect are complicated and inherently inconclusive, there are *some* parallels between Roman times and ours. Various analogies, however trite or inaccurate in their usual formulations, ought not be dismissed without some thought, at least as sources for conjectures. . . .

FUNCTIONS OF WORK

To arrive more precisely at an answer to the question, "What are the consequences of a reduction in the amount of work that needs to be done?" one must ask, "What are the various functions for the individual of the work he performs?" It is easy to make a long list of such benefits at various levels of analysis. For example, people derive from work such benefits as role; status; sense of striving; feeling of productivity, competency, and achievement; and relationships with others and advancement in a hierarchy, whether organizational or professional.

[Table 3] shows some rough characterizations and generalizations about various roles work may play for different kinds of people in the year 2000. Those whose basic attitude toward work is that it is totally abhorrent or reprehensible are not listed, since on the whole they will find it possible to avoid employment entirely.

As discussed later one could easily imagine that many Americans from "normal" (i.e., not deprived) backgrounds will increasingly adopt the first position, that work is an interruption, while many formerly in the lower and economically depressed classes will increasingly shift to the second or third positions which reflect more work-oriented and achievement-oriented values. On the other hand,

Table 3

Basic Attitude Toward Work As:	Basic Additional Value Fulfilled by Work
1. Interruption	Short-run income
2. Job	Long-term income—some work-oriented values (one works to live)
3. Occupation	Exercise and mastery of gratifying skills— some satisfaction of achievement-oriented values
4. Career	Participating in an important activity or program. Much satisfaction of work-oriented, achievement-oriented, advancement-oriented values
5. Vocation (calling)	Self-identification and self-fulfillment
6. Mission	Near fanatic or single-minded focus on achievement or advancement (one lives to work)

the man whose missionary zeal for work takes priority over all other values will be looked on as an unfortunate, perhaps even a harmful and destructive neurotic. Even those who find in work a "vocation" are likely to be thought of as selfish, excessively narrow, or compulsive.

Many of the benefits of work could be derived from other forms of activity, provided they were available and, preferably, institutionalized. The model of the cultivated gentlemen, for example, is likely to be available and possibly generally usable in a democratic and upward mobile society like the United States. It may be argued that aristocrats are far more visible in Europe and that it is more respectable for the wealthy to live as landed gentry, rentiers, even as playboys in Europe than in the United States, and that for these reasons the transition to this pattern of life would be easier in Europe. Indeed, historically this has often been the aspiration and achievement (after a generation or two) of the upper middle class and even the lower class nouveaux riches. On the other hand, if it became the ideal it is probably more difficult for a typical European to think of making the social transition to such a status for himself than it would be for the typical American. Of course, the American has seen fewer examples of such lives, and has up to now respected them less. Therefore it seems less likely to be the American ideal.

In the economic structure we are describing, there may be a special problem of the service professions whose productivity per hour may not have gone up. Thus many believe there are probably important limits to the extent to which the efficiency of persons such as teachers, professors, doctors, lawyers, ministers, psychologists, social workers, and so forth can be increased. Others believe that not only can these professions be automated,[8] but that there are huge opportunities for increasing efficiency through better organization, specialization, and the very skilled use of computers. Nevertheless, there are likely to remain irreducible kinds of activities that defy rationalization or improvement, such as those that require face-to-face meeting and conversation. Thus programmed instruction, lectures, and sermons over television are not likely to displace face-to-face human communication, at least not without great loss to those involved. Therefore only part of the current activity in these fields is likely to increase in productivity.

To the extent that recruitment into the service professions is greatly expanded because of the reduced need for people in manufacturing, routine aspects of public administration, and automated administrative and managerial tasks, several problems will arise. One is that it will be perhaps more difficult to recruit people to do difficult and demanding work that either requires long and arduous training or requires working under difficult, dangerous, or frustrating conditions. If the hours of work of people in these professions go down severely, the incentives and psychological functions of membership in the profession may be somewhat diluted. For example, a hospital may have three head nurses if there are three shifts; what happens, however, when there are six or eight shifts? To what extent is authority, expertise, and satisfaction diluted when power, responsibility, and status are so fractionated?

Similar questions should be posed about other kinds of activities. In general, a threefold increase in GNP per capita is far from the equivalent of a threefold increase in productivity per capita in all relevant respects. As real productivity increases dramatically in certain industries, principally in manufacturing and heavily clerical industries, such as banking and insurance and many federal, state, and local governmental functions, which could be very much auto-

[8] Thus much legal research can be done most easily through a computerized library. A physician may be able to phone a list of symptoms into a central computer and get back a print-out of suggested diagnostic possibilities. Many laboratory tests might be performable by methods which would present immediate results. Closed circuit television and various kinds of continuously reading tests presented on central display boards could even now make the utilization of hospital personnel also much more efficient. Other possibilities were mentioned in Chapter II [*The Year 2000*].

mated, the price structure would also change dramatically. This would result in enormous increase in the availability, variety, and quality of goods and many standardized services, since these items would become very much cheaper or very much better for the same price. A threefold increase in GNP per capita would probably imply a much greater increase in standard of living with respect to these items. Yet, at the same time, skilled, personal services requiring irreducible quantities of human time, training, and talent would become both absolutely and relatively expensive. Thus there would probably still be a very strong demand for, and probably also a much expanded supply of expensive and skilled professionals, managers, entrepreneurs, artisans, technicians and artists—for the most part, the well-educated upper middle class. This group may well be much too busy and well rewarded to be alienated.

Furthermore, even if one imagines the ordinary member of the labor force amply supplied with intricate technology affording innumerable needs and luxuries during his short work week, and even if he can travel anywhere in the less-developed world and easily buy vast quantities of domestic service and other personal attentions during his long vacations, many important consumer items are likely to remain too expensive for him to wish his work week to become *too* short. There will probably still be a class of "luxury items," consisting of such things as vacation houses in extremely exotic places, advanced or "sporty" personal vehicles such as perhaps ground-effect machines, or similar items for the most part well beyond today's technology and prohibitively expensive for ordinary workers by today's standards, that by the year 2000 will be still expensive, but perhaps within reach of the man who is interested in earning enough money—and many, no doubt, will be interested.

Chapter 15

misused technology: humanity as a cog in the machine

Jacques Ellul

Work techniques began with the world of the machine and displayed scant regard for human beings. Machines were invented and assembled, buildings were put up around them, and men were put inside. For fifty years the procedure was completely haphazard. Then it was noted that the worker's productivity could be markedly increased by imposing certain rules on him. The result was the system associated with the names of the Americans Frederick Winslow Taylor and Henry Ford. As Georges Friedmann has shown, they took nothing into consideration beyond the necessities of production and the maximum utilization of the machine; they completely ignored the serfdom these factors entail—with their production lines, their infinite subdivision of tasks, and so on.

The objection will be raised, and rightly so, that this system was gradually changed and eventually became concerned not so much with questions of maximal exploitation as with optimal results. Worker fatigue (a topic we still don't know enough about) became the subject of intense investigations. The importance of the human factor was recognized. And it even began to be recognized that this was insufficient, that man was still only one "factor" among many, and not the most important. It became necessary to recognize the primacy of the whole human being, to adapt the work to the man, and to take the worker's psychological equilibrium into consideration. It goes without saying that the motive force behind all this was the recognition that human psychology reacts directly upon productivity. When the worker feels that he is in a hostile environment and in an economic system opposed to his interests, he will not work (and this is involuntary) with the same ardor and skill. All this, according to Friedmann, posed the problem of the economic regime as a whole. Economic improvement is not of itself a strong enough tendency to allow the worker as producer to benefit from technical progress, although he may have benefited greatly from it as consumer. Purely material transformations in the conditions of labor are insufficient. They are doubtless necessary to begin with, but physiological adaptation is not the only kind. Hygiene and safety must indeed be improved; the best location must be selected, and even music may have to be exploited to make labor more rhythmic and less disagreeable. But this is still not enough. The true problem is psychological. The worker is confronted by cut-and-dried procedures that must be carried out in unvarying sequence in order that work be systematic, rational, and efficient; he is bored, slowed down, and psychologically constrained. It is necessary to arouse in him reflective thought and to make him participate in the life of the entire plant. He must be made to feel a community of interest; the idea that his labor has social meaning must be instilled in him. In short, he must be integrated into the enterprise in which he is working. This integration will take different forms in different countries. It may take the form of a manufacturing structure like that of Bata,[1] or it may consist of social, sports, or educational arrangements. Integration may mean worker participation in finance or management or, in an extreme case, the application of a thorough system such as "public relations" or "human engineering." It suffices here to point out some of the many techniques of integration without going into their quite varied mechanisms.

Some excellent results have been achieved along this line. For example, the tendency to adapt the machine to man and to assert man's primacy over the machine has produced a body of respectable research. Until recently, very few designers and manufacturers of machine tools bothered much about the workers who were to use the tools. It represents enormous progress for them to acknowledge that machines should be built with the workers in mind, that the human being ought to be the point of departure. However, the further they advance in this direction, the more complicated the problem appears. They were at first concerned primarily with the elimination of physical fatigue; having succeeded in this, they find that nervous or mental fatigue is now a problem. Business machines are highly adapted to the worker from a material point of view;

---

[1] Thomas Bata (1876–1932) was a Czech industrialist who made his shoe factories at Zlin into a federation of independent "studios." (Trans.)

physical effort has been almost completely reduced by the progressive elimination of fatigue due to standing, sensory overburdening, and the need for overtime work. But the reduction of physical effort has only served to increase fatigue due to mental concentration, reflex attention, and dissymmetry of motion, factors which rapidly produce nervous exhaustion. It was certainly not anticipated that machines designed for man, and well adapted to him physically, would occasion even more rapid deterioration and an accelerated aging of their operators. Indeed, worker productivity markedly decreases after only four years, and, in general, becomes marked at age twenty-two. The optimum age of an employee who operates business machines would seem to lie between sixteen and twenty-two. Now, this last fact comes from the machine in itself, from its tempo, and so on. The human problem has been intensified, rather than resolved. It even seems insoluble. The concern for the human being that is evident in these attempts must, one supposes, be reckoned progress; the same holds for the technician's concern with the person of the worker, and the attempts to furnish him with means for self-improvement by establishing libraries or by helping him resolve his personal problems.

But on further consideration, are not these efforts and this interest part of an abstract ideal? What do they really signify? Leon Walther, the great theoretician of the adaptation of machine to man, states that this adaptation has as its end "the maximum productivity with the minimum expenditure of human energy." But such a goal represents a primary of efficiency, with reference both to man and machine. The greater concern is to make men work effectively; and, marvelous dispensation, advantages for production turn out to coincide with advantages for the individual.

One of the principal creators of libraries for workers has described the concept of "practical utility" which ought to govern such libraries. Books are to be selected on the basis of "their eventual moral yield." If a book enables the worker to escape the direct control of the bosses, "it ought to be authorized only to the degree that the subject treated allows the management to exercise control indirectly." With this proviso, a book can be an invaluable auxiliary, since it introduces personal interest, serves as a source of initiative, and satisfies curiosity; but on the condition that the worker is ignorant of what he ought to know and that management has the "duty" to choose for him.

It might, incidentally, be asked: "Are these ideas capitalist or Communist?" Anyone who could give an unambiguous answer to this question would indeed be an expert, for the same conceptions occur as frequently in one system as in the other. They do not represent theories, but are the direct expression of the fact that work technique necessitates the complete integration of the worker. It is inadmissible that the worker's reading matter should occasion slowdowns, rebellion, or displacement of the center of interest. Such things are unthinkable, whatever the regime. Culture must conform to technique and encourage productivity. Censorship in this area ought therefore not to be regarded as an evil, but as an unavoidable condition of objective technique. The same holds for the surprising creation of the post of "counselors," of which Friedmann has written. After it had been observed in certain industrial plants that the conditions of modern labor provoke psychological difficulties, psychologists were hired to act as "safety valves" for employee grievances and dissatisfactions. Employees may express their feelings to these "counselors" with the assurance that the counselors will say nothing to management. But the counselors never actually counsel anything. Their activities have nothing whatever to do with a positive cure of the soul, a mission which would suppose at least the possibility of profound changes, new orientations, and an awakening consciousness on the worker's part, all of which are highly dangerous. Nor are the counselors concerned with investigations of concrete modifications that might be binding on the company. Their sole duty is to encourage the voicing of complaints and to listen to them. It is well-known that suffering expressed is suffering relieved. It has been observed that certain psychological disturbances are provoked simply by being silent and that rebellions are nourished in secret. To let people talk does them good and quashes revolt. It is dangerous to allow the workers to talk over their problems among themselves. It is far more prudent to give them a safety valve in the form of a discreet company agent, a psychological technician, than to let them air their grievances in public. These "counselors" play the same role on the industrial level as the Soviet magazine *Krokodil* does on the political. It is difficult to find a human interest in any of this. The concern here is primarily with technical development. The palliation of the human difficulties raised by technique is secondary. Michel Crozier asserts that this is true also for the technique called "human engineering."

This situation exists also in other disciplines (for example, in sociology), which forces us to conclusions that seem in no sense subjective. Social research establishes the primacy of the sociological over the human: it is not concerned only with man's individual psychology and physiology, but also with his relation to the body social. Here the important problem is to make him really belong to the social group. The problem is the same for a socialized as for a capitalist economy. A solution may perhaps be more feasible for a capitalist society, but both are faced with the problem of convincing man and gaining his allegiance. This gives rise to yet another human technique, which I shall refer to later on. At this point let us consider its aims.

In *Aspects sociaux de la rationalisation,* the 1931 report of the International Labor Organization, we read that "it is necessary to rationalize not only manufacturing, but also employer-employee relations." And in 1941 the ILO asserted that "only when industrial technique succeeds in developing concern for the human being will American capitalism win the confidence of its workers, customers, and bond holders, of the public individually and collectively." As Friedmann puts it, the purpose of the scientific organization of labor, before and after the advent of psychotechnique, industrial relations, and technical humanism, was and is to "assure maximal yield with minimal loss of effort or material. But these latter represent means which are becoming complicated and refined to the point of transforming little by little the face of the scientific organization of labor." The system of human relations which is being re-created in the industrial framework is constructed, according to its originators, on the basis of an industrial model. In this respect the study of W. E. Moore is significant. According to Moore, human relations must correspond to the functions of individuals engaged in the production cycle. Moore assigns the following four characteristics to human relations:

First, human relations must be restricted to the technical demands of their vocational role. They must not become deep relations involving profound ideas, tendencies, and preoccupations. Individuals who are part of the industrial tempo must remain human and sustain mutual human relationships, but only those that relate to technical activity.

Second, human relations must be universal; they must be "based on criteria which the members of an arbitrary grouping of the population can satisfy, independently of prior social relations or prior membership in other groups unconnected with the work in hand." In other words, human relations must not have an extra-technical basis. The individual's prior milieu is of little importance; neither are his prior preferences or tendencies. Technique compensates for everything else. It is therefore reasonable to speak of technical "universalism." Technique is the bond between men; it is both objective and indeterminate; it makes up for individual deficiencies, admitting no excuses or individual dissociation.

The third characteristic of human relations is rationality. Human relations are indispensable to the proper functioning of the organism as a whole. The organism is strictly rational, and relations integrated into it must be conceived on a rational basis. Emotion or sentimentality must not be allowed to disturb the mechanism. When the problem of emotion is considered, as, for example, in "molar microsociological analysis," it is treated as a function of the greater rationality of the group and of a more objective equilibrium.

In the fourth place, these relations must be impersonal, established not on the basis of subjective choice and for personal reasons but on the basis of their optimum validity. Of course, subjective choice and personal reasons must also be dealt with insofar as they influence the technician, but they are stripped of spontaneous validity; they are only one element in the situation.

Scott and Lynton, in a rather more versatile study made in 1953, confirm Moore's analysis. According to them, in the technical complex which our society has become, and which is destroying every kind of community, it is necessary to compensate for man's natural incapacity to sustain human relations in a technical universe. This must be done not only for man's sake but also because human relations are technically indispensable to the progress of great enterprises. It is necessary, therefore, to organize groups in these enterprises, groups which are responsible but also sufficiently directed to serve the common end, productivity. Then it is necessary to reproduce natural conditions artificially, so that human relations can be established. For example, the enterprise can be given an administrative structure that reproduces a spontaneous organization.

The technique of so-called human relations, developed to adapt the individual to the technical milieu, to force him to accept his slavery, to make him find happiness by the "normalization" of his relations with his group and integrate him into that group to an ever greater degree—this technique is characteristic of the fakeries and shams with which men must be provided if the conflicts provoked by life in a technicized environment are to be avoided. As a remedy it does not amount to much, but as a symptom of technical reinforcement, it is important. We can say that these personal relations are also techniques, that they are not a counterweight to other techniques, but that they bring about the application of technique in the most personal and immediate area of human activities: man's relations with other men. They alleviate the rigors of the human condition—but only by forcing man to submit to them more completely. They facilitate both human life and the action of the machinery, improve production while subordinating human spontaneity to the mathematical calculations of the technicians. In short, they are a kind of lubricating oil, but scarcely a means by which men can recover a sense of worth, personality, and authenticity. On the contrary, they are a delusion which desiccate the individual's desire for anything better. Man is doubtless made more comfortable by techniques of human relations; but these techniques are wholly oriented toward compelling man to submit to forced labor. Machine and productivity are in the driver's seat.

Chapter 16

the counter-culture thrust:
living poor with style

Ernest Callenbach

POOR IS "IN"

An unexpected crisis has come upon America. We have finally realized that the rosy picture of life given us in the fifties and sixties by magazines and newspapers and politicians is false. . . .

This failure of the old American way is naturally generating a new life-style, arising to challenge the old. Millions of young people who grew up in the rank atmosphere of warfare-state "affluence" have seen the consequences of that way—and found it wanting. They are not sure what they want instead, but they know what they don't want.

They don't want to be the unwilling backers of troops in costly and immoral foreign wars. They don't want to be obedient consumers, salivating like Pavlov's dogs before an advertisement. They don't want to work at meaningless jobs—producing junk or shuffling a corporation's bureaucratic papers—in order to buy more stuff from which neither they nor their families nor their friends get any real joy. They want to be free men and women. And to be that, they are willing to be poor: to drop out of the corporations and universities and official culture and instead try building up a life-style that will suit them. This can mean scrounging, scavenging, welfare, do-it-yourself, subsistence farming, communes, odd jobs, part-time jobs. It's not an easy life. But it can be a real and personal and satisfying life—fit for a man to live. . . .

THE COVETOUS SOCIETY

The Ten Commandments tell us that we are not to covet our neighbor's wife, or his goods. If we took this seriously, modern business would collapse in a day. The very foundation of contemporary society is covetousness. We are trained to covet practically from the day of birth.

If we get into situations where there is nothing around to covet, we get nervous—like first-time campers, or tourists in East European countries who wonder why there aren't more downtown shop windows. We are, in fact, conditioned exactly like trained rats in a maze. Galvanized into action by a paycheck, we nose around, hunting for the ultimate purchase which will satisfy our hunger. Since most of us never have enough money for more than a few of the available toys, we are spared the dreadful realization that comes to the rich: there really isn't that much worth coveting. We go on busily and endlessly sniffing after the bait, and finally we drop dead in the maze, without ever stopping to consider whose game we have been playing.

In order to stop coveting, it may be necessary to be able to enjoy a lot of goods for a while. At any rate, this seems to be why the majority of hippies are from middle-class backgrounds: they've seen all their parents' toys and had a lot of their own, and they know by experience (which is how we learn almost everything we ever learn) that coveting is a bum trip. To people who all their lives have been deprived of the goodies enjoyed by the middle classes and the rich, the suggestion of doing without sounds like the old recommendation from rich people that the poor should enjoy being poor and honest.

But if coveting is your trip, you should at least try to get through it as quickly as possible. Work your ass off, put your money into all the goodies you can manage, spend your time in stores, read *Consumer Reports*, talk to experts: really sink yourself into it for a while.

Then kick it, and get back to figuring out what you really want to do with your life.

Every culture, like every person's life, has both a material and a spiritual side. In the development of an American counterculture, much of the ground clearing has already been done: we have rejected the decadent national values of militarism, unbridled

polluting technology, and the obnoxious pursuit of individual profit
at the expense of the people at large.

We are not yet so certain about how we *do* wish to live.
However, many new philosophical and political ideas are busily
threading their way through our society. Some people who reject
the anti-sex and anti-nature bias of Western "civilization" turn to
Zen or other kinds of Buddhism which emphasize man's existence
as part of nature, and encourage simplicity and directness in living.
Some people who reject the authoritarian relationships inherent in
modern business and even in electoral democracy turn to anar-
chism—which is not a doctrine of chaos, but an elaborate political
theory based on the assumption that man is just as capable of
living in relative peace without a coercive social structure as other
animals are. People who are disgusted at the rape of the landscape
caused by industrial society sometimes turn back to the American
Indians for inspiration about how to live on the land without
wrecking it—gathering wild foods, living in portable houses. Some
people study other so-called "primitive" cultures for ideas about
how man can achieve a better ecological balance with his environment. And some people, by experimenting with drugs that affect
perception or produce visions, attempt to get in touch with the
underlying realities of their own minds—or at least to escape the
dead routines of the conventional thinking they have been taught.

Living has to do with how you eat and sleep and where you
live and with whom; with how you relate to jobs and money; with
machinery, furniture, and other objects; with how you dress; with
how you deal with the law, the government, the police, the army.
To every habit and convention of the old American culture, we
are developing counter-patterns and counter-habits—anti-habits,
sometimes, or the rejection of any habits at all, in favor of a fluidity
from which new things may come.

So far the new ways have only begun to challenge the old.
But already they have aroused the fears and resistances commonly
stirred up by revolutionary thinking. The new ways have a powerful
attraction, and they are spreading out from our tumultuous cities
throughout the land. Their outward signs have begun to appear even
in small cities and towns: brighter clothes, longer hair, funky old
cars, rock music, drugs, organic and unsprayed foods, freer sexual
relationships. Like a vast tribe of wandering Gypsies, people freed
from the old conventions are spreading out.

Some preach the gospel to willing (and sometimes unwilling)
ears. Some prefer to live quietly, letting the force of their example
serve. Some are political, ready to argue how the miserable, desperate

psychological condition of middle-class life is the result of the needs of the giant corporations and the military-industrial elite which controls them—and how American foreign policy is an extension abroad of these oppresssive policies. Some are mystical, believing that only by putting your own soul in order, through meditation or drugs or religion, can you hope to live a contented life. But through all these variations of emphasis there runs a common disdain for the traditional American way—the life of work-work-work, buy-buy-buy.

And slowly, even among the squarest of citizens, the suspicion is growing that it is the very nature of our vastly developed industrial system to produce an environment which is poisonous to our bodies and toxic to our minds. Perhaps the making and buying of goods is *not* the main goal of a sane society. Perhaps a bigger Gross National Product is not a god worth sacrificing our lives to. Perhaps we must question the whole orientation of American values. The early labor-union leader Sam Gompers once summed up the aims of the labor movement as "More!" But maybe now we need less—and better?

Paradoxically, this question is being asked just when millions of black Americans are making a strong push to get what has been denied them since slavery. Black revolutionaries see this trend toward acquisitiveness as evil because it obscures the fact that the black population as a whole is still getting poorer relative to the white population. It seems clear, at any rate, that poor people of all races must stand together and organize politically to bring about a new life of real freedom and equality. . . .

What is different about the present moment is that modern education and mass communications have made practically everybody realize that we now have the resources and the technology to provide a decent living for all. And for the first time in history, sizable masses of people are deciding that a decent modest living is all they want: they are leaving the middle-class money chase and *deciding* to be poor—not miserably poor, of course, but poorer in money so they can be richer in time, in enjoyments, in living a life that makes sense to human beings instead of to machines and accountants.

DANGEROUS DOUBTS

Changing your life in this way means questioning many of the old ideals Americans have thought they had to live by.

Take *labor saving*, for example. Saving the labor of walking or bicycling by riding around in cars all the time has put Americans into probably the worst physical shape of any nation on earth. Saving labor by buying precooked or prefabricated foods not only makes your diet less interesting, but it may actually make you work *harder:* you have to work about ten extra minutes at your job to earn the difference between a cake made from a mix and a scratch cake. And the scratch cake will contain no preservatives or other suspect chemicals; besides, it will taste better, and will give you the pleasure of having done something satisfying for yourself, in just the way you want it.

Take *technological progress.* For years we have been told about the wonders of modern science. But it is now clear that much of our proud progress is illusory—and that many of our supposed advances do at least as much harm as good. Thus, for instance, chemical insecticides like DDT were welcomed as miracles of chemistry that would save crops from every kind of bug. It has taken us twenty years to realize that DDT kills some bugs but gives free rein to others, so that an orchard may be saved from peach borers but is then overrun with tiny mites. Worse still, DDT accumulates in water, in vegetables, in animals and fish. In 1969 it was discovered that Lake Michigan salmon were so full of DDT they were dangerous to eat. Human breast milk contains so much DDT that if it were bottled it would be illegal to ship it across state lines. (It is still better than cow's milk, however.) DDT has even led to the virtual extermination of several bird species whose eggshells are becoming too fragile to hatch.

Much of the new technology, then, seems to be bad for the human race, and we should subject all innovations to careful, personal, human, and ecological checks. If a new device contributes to the ugliness, impersonality, dirt, heat, noise, garbage, and air pollution of the world, we ought to reject it. Certainly we should keep it out of our houses. . . .

Take *cleanliness.* American have a fetish for washing. They buy staggering quantities of soaps and detergents and are constantly washing themselves, their children, their cars, their clothes. They tend to feel that unless a thing shines there must be something wicked about it. But biologically, man does not take well to all this shininess. Soaps and detergents wreck his skin and hair and give him rashes. Shiny cars hurt his eyes on the highways; his cities are so glaring he has to wear sunglasses. Having varnished or lacquered or polished everything, he is deprived of the variations in texture and pattern which occur in the natural world for which evolution prepared him.

Even natural smells are suppressed. Does anyone really want to smell another person who is "soapy-clean"? Our sense of smell happens to be a highly personal and immensely powerful emotional force; whether we like it or not, we are extremely sensitive to the smells of our families, our lovers, our households, our own bodies. Americans are willing to admit that babies smell nice, but that's about all. Basically, the American tradition is anti-biological. . . .

Take the idea of *"new."* The American mania for newness is drummed into us to convince us that our old things can't be any good, and we'd better hurry up and earn some money to replace them. But the new ones probably won't be as much fun to use as the old. They'll break down quicker, they are almost sure to be uglier, and they cost a hell of a lot more. A handy rule for a saner life is this: If you are lucky enough to possess something you like that's lasted for more than a couple of years, hang on to it. You'll probably never find a new one half as good.

Take the concept of the *nuclear family*. Earlier Americans lived in "extended-family" groups—a dwelling contained not only a father, mother, and children, but probably an aunt or uncle or so, probably a grandfather or grandmother, and possibly nephews, cousins, or other relatives. Houses were, on the whole, larger in those days, though many city people lived in slum tenements as they do now.

Today a family is supposed to consist of only two parents and their children. Grandparents are shoved off into rest homes or left to live by themselves. Everybody who is single is expected to provide for himself or herself. The present way has its advantages, as anybody with a senile parent will quickly point out. But it is on the whole a colder, more impersonal way. Like many other aspects of the American traditional pattern, it puts people into closer touch with machines, but removes them from human contact.

Modern young people are less and less convinced that the nuclear family pattern is habitable, and they are therefore experimenting with communal living, both in the cities and countryside. These experiments are usually attempted by people who are not related to each other except through common experience: drugs, disillusionment with the university, political or religious consciousness. Some communes share vegetarian food practices. Some who have rejected the whole idea of city living turn to American Indian ways. There are many disagreements in and between communes, for once you cast off the old ideas, many new ones spring up, and it takes time to test them. Like the two-person family or any other human arrangement where people are in extended contact and intimacy with each other, communes are not havens of peace and tranquillity. (As is well known, the best way to be perfectly tranquil is to be dead.)

The old extended-family pattern was based on two things: blood relationship and economic necessity. The big family enabled the individual to spend less money, have more pleasures, and be better protected against the dangers of life. Today, we like to ignore the dangers and imagine that science or the police have conquered them. However, as Americans become more realistic, they are becoming aware of their own vulnerability: they know that they will need help against disease, accident, crime, poverty, death, and their own families are often far away—at the other end of the country, or off at war. Commune dwellers, thus, are trying to see whether the bonds of common ideas and common needs are strong enough to sustain new kinds of groupings, where say ten to thirty people, often including permanent or married couples and children, live together and share housing, food, child raising, and so on.

The economic advantages are impressive. Let's take a group of only ten persons—three couples, two children, and two single persons. (This is roughly the minimum size of another stable social grouping—the wolf pack.) Under the conventional way of life they would have to rent five separate apartments or houses; as a commune they rent one large house or very large apartment. Each day, under the old system, fifteen separate meals would have to be prepared— and at a far greater cost than if all the cooking were done in one place. Costs for laundry, heating, lights, and so on will be far less per person than if separate dwellings are maintained. Even if each couple or person has individual radio/TVs, typewriters, irons, and other small items of personal property, it is possible on the average to live in a commune for less than half of what the old way requires. For many people existing on welfare, unemployment, disability, or retirement incomes, this can mean the difference between pleasant survival and utter poverty. . . .

Many communes, especially in rural areas, have been started on ambitious scales. Often rural groups plan to be self-sufficient concerning food, shelter, and clothing—though the land to live on generally comes from a family inheritance, a gift, or some other outside source. Some communes are positively puritanical, with rigid work duties, obligatory ceremonies, and careful planning of every aspect of life—totally opposite from the middle-class view of communes as permanent round-the-clock orgies. However, a former country dweller like myself knows that subsistence farming is extremely difficult to survive on in this country no matter how hardworking the communards may be. City kids who don't know a ewe from a moo will obviously have a very hard time, but so will handy, skilled, and reasonably lucky people who take advantage of every agricultural advance and work doggedly. The fact is that to produce all your food and even part of your clothing through individual farming takes such large amounts of energy that very few Americans are up to it. Every commune that hopes to endure, therefore, needs some steady, though perhaps not very large source of outside income —occasional or part-time jobs, welfare, or whatever. This will make it possible to divert some energies to the production of things which are unavailable commercially in the desired quality, or things which are overpriced commercially, things which can be produced with little money risked.

RESOURCES FOR THE NEW WAYS

There is as yet no solid, effective, comfortable style of living poor in this country. Instead of working out ways of living that are suitable for human beings who are free, we tend to straggle along in the foul exhausts of the advertisers. . . .

CONSUMERISM, SCRIMPING, AND OTHER BUM TRIPS

Newspapers and magazines abound with advice about how to "save" money by spending it wisely—how to be a smarter consumer. Some advice of this kind can be useful, and there is some of it in this book. But the real point is to *stop being a consumer*—that is to say, a creature whose social role is to buy stuff. A "consumer" is a kind of servant of the industrial society. It produces tons of lettuce, he eats lettuce, perhaps selecting one type over another. It produces hair dryers; he buys hair dryers, studiously comparing brand names. In short, he is playing the corporations' game.

You only really save money, and time, and your freedom, by *not* buying—ultimately, by "paying" attention not to what they are trying to get you to pay attention to, but to things that personally matter to you.

It is not easy to discover what personally matters to you. By the time a kid is six or eight, he has been exposed to thousands of hours of television commercials. And by the time he has finished high school, he has been thoroughly brainwashed into thinking about (and wanting) all the stuff that has been presented on TV, in magazines, and in the households of fellow brainwashed citizens.

We must stop being consumers and become *producers:* producers of ideas, of friendships, of beautiful objects, of better relationships among all people, of a more humane and decent society.

One of the chief secrets of learning to live well without much money is that it is bad to scrimp. Penny-pinching is bad for the spirit. Few of the ideas in this book involve the mean and depressing kind of trim-here and squeeze-there budgeting often recommended to people without enough money. Instead, the wise and free person recognizes that buying things (with all the cost consciousness and calculation it involves) is not the central question. The central question is *how to organize your life.* If you decide to organize it by your own standards and desires and needs, you will find that buying takes on an entirely different aspect.

For one thing, you will come to know what your necessities really are. Obviously these will include food and shelter and clothes —possibly on a more modest scale than you tended to think. But they may also include music, or flowers or a southern-exposure window; privacy or an open-door policy; lots of heat or lots of fresh air; bright lights or dim.

Furthermore, you will discover that buying is not the only and often not a desirable way to obtain things. St. Francis is said to have remarked that to beg is best, to steal is next, and to buy is worst of all. This doctrine tends to appeal most to those who crave the excitement of stealing. But I would think that the saintly bird lover did not sufficiently study his birds: to a bird, begging, stealing, and buying are all irrelevant terms; and in this and other respects we can learn by watching our fellow animals who have not been corrupted by speech or ideas.

American Indians too once lived upon the land like birds— taking what they needed, but without destroying the fabric of plant and animal life which produced it. The "taking" was hard—as anyone knows who has tried to subsist even a short time by hunting and gathering food, or who has tried to construct a shelter and implements without machine-made tools. And it is an aristocratic illusion, usually held by people with unearned income from parents or inheritances, that men can live in any numbers without a good deal of hard work. Occasional saints (or sinners) bring it off, but they are isolated persons for whom the essentials of life—some bread, a roof at night, some wine—can indeed be begged, or borrowed, or shoplifted. The real problem in modern industrial society, capitalist or socialist, is that we must work *for others,* not for ourselves. When we seek money by offering our time and energy in the labor market we are putting ourselves at the disposal of others, and the purposes of the work we are assigned are often so remote they have no meaning.

We do need money to buy food and shelter. Still, by redirecting our energies, we may find that we need to *buy* far less and can *make* far more.

This also saves money: instead of paying $75 for a bed in a furniture store, you can make one for $25. But that is only a fringe benefit. What counts most is that instead of working for someone else over the hours needed to produce that extra $50, you were working for yourself, in your own place, with your own companions, at your own pace, with your own ideas and designs and materials and tools. The resulting bed is *your* bed—in a way no Simmons bed could ever be.

Calling themselves consumers, modern Americans are literally consumed by the industrial system—and on two fronts: they must sacrifice to it their alienated labor, to get money; and to get food, shelter, and other needs they are confined in the maw of the marketplace, which offers many choices but only with the exchange of money. Thus money becomes the measure of all things, including your life: all goods and all people become cost-rated commodities. While the US government rates a Vietnamese civilian killed "by accident" at a few thousand dollars (if anything), a good wage-earner run down by a truck at home may be worth a hundred thousand—as defined by his potential earning power, or perhaps his insurance policies. When such standards become widespread, the value of human life *in itself* is forgotten. All life is consumed by "the cash nexus," as Marx called it—the bargaining act by which every thing and person is weighed at somebody's cash register.

We can escape the cash nexus only to the extent we escape dealing with cash.

Thus in this [chapter] many ideas are put forward not as ways to "save money" but to avoid dealing with it altogether. What I hope to do is to show that a whole system of attitudes and practices exists, in embryonic form, which can help us combat our fatal dependence on the cash nexus—and thus give us the courage and strength to use our own powers, our own imaginations, directly on our own behalf. We need to live with our own hands, to control our own beings. In a world where everything from a steam shovel to a coffin can be rented and cost-accounted and deducted from income taxes, we must defend our own life spaces, lest we find ourselves rented too.

In the full-blown industrial state such as we inhabit, the "duties" of the citizen are to work steadily and obediently, pay taxes and union dues, vote when called upon, consume enough goods to keep the economy going, and occasionally trot off to the other side of the world to fight for some dictatorial regime and save the national face. We must struggle politically to defend ourselves from such a well-organized fate—let them build robots! But in order to struggle we must also and at the same time develop a different way of living: of eating and sleeping, of loving, of traveling about, of educating ourselves and our children, of amusing ourselves, of securing medical care and political redress. The old-style American way of life has been gobbled up by the industrial age, and spat out upon the ruined landscape. What we must do now is build a counter-culture, a new Way.

The problems we face, in trying to make modern America habitable for human beings again, are not to any serious degree technical. They are problems of *holiness*: we are searching for ways of restoring dignity and importance to daily events. It is, in a sense, a religious quest. We have to relearn how to pay true attention to what we are doing, because there is little solid pleasure in things done thoughtlessly or mechanically. We must learn to eat holy, dress holy, smoke holy, wash holy, and so on.

Since organized religion has abandoned the people, people must create their own religion. The beginning seems to lie in something rather like the American Indian's concept of "medicine." The things we use and wear, if we make them with care and use them with respect, take on "good medicine"; they become holy because of the sincerity of our regard for them and the extent of our commitment to them. It is hard for disposable goods to be holy. When we buy manufactured goods, even of honest quality (which is hard to find), it is always doubtful whether our spirit can enter into them. Best of all are those things which are old, have been well loved, and have become holy through association with people we love and respect: ancestors, old friends, great men or women.

It is very hard to find the right way, and no person should lightly despise another's way. Out of the welter of present industrial society, it will probably take us several generations to sort out those few things which are essential to mankind—and to reject the others, of which no truly human or holy use can be made. We should be patient with each other's experiments, but cleave to our task, now that we know what it is; it leaves little room for cant or credulity.

Chapter 17

technology and utopia

Carolyn Symonds

The question frequently arises as to whether or not Utopia, by
definition, requires a retreat to the past. Many of the communes,
and groups of people who gather together or retreat by themselves,
whether indicating a religious or secular philosophy, feel that the
evils of the world have come about because of industrialization.
They attempt to retreat into a past that seems more Utopian than
the present or the foreseeable future. Would it not instead be possible to build a Utopia utilizing the technological advantages
brought about by industrialization?

> Webster's definition of Utopia is: an imaginary country with ideal
> laws and social conditions 1: a place (as a region, island, country, or
> locality) that is imaginary and indefinitely remote; 2: *often caps:* a
> place, state, or condition of ideal perfection, esp. in laws, govern-
> ment, and social conditions.[1]

From Carolyn Symonds, "Technology and Utopia," in *The Modern Utopian: Modern Man in Search of Utopia,* ed. Richard Fairfield (San Francisco:
Alternatives Foundation, 1971), pp. 9–11.

[1] *Webster's Third New International Dictionary, Unabridged.* G. & C. Mer-
riam Co., Mass., 1961. This is the current and popularized definition of "utopia."
The original root meaning is no (u) place (topia) from the Latin. Just as all great
religious thoughts have been bastardized by their followers so has "utopia" by its.
People like to put things outside themselves but the "ideal state" is not an institution but within the self. There can never be "ideal laws and social conditions . . . a place of ideal perfection." That's a contradiction in terms and contrary to everything we experience in life (the laws of nature—ugh). We can
improve laws, institutions, social conditions, but make them perfect *for everyone?*
While utopia is not-a-place, nowhere—now here—we as individuals, can get
much closer to it. Even shit is a part of utopia—sanitation regulations are not
essential. And, yes, pain, too, can be a part of utopia. The perfect state is not
that of a contented cow chewing on her cud.—Ed. [Richard Fairfield]

There is nothing in this definition that implies a step into the past. People view life in the past as more Utopian than the present and mechanization is seen as the villain to be rejected. However, I would like to propose a society built on the utilization of technology.

My response to the question has been greatly influenced by R. Buckminister Fuller[2] and his discussion of the direction of technological change and the ultimate capabilities of modern technology. He brings out two points that are very important and need to be mentioned.

The first is the concept of more-with-lessing. In effect, the greatest technological impact on society is the application of the principle of doing more with less. He says that no new mining would have to be accomplished to support the entire world population if reclamation was made of previously worked materials, if the more-with-less concept was consciously developed.

The other point he makes is that our present war technology (where most technological development occurs) is such that humanity will be in the bind of having to secure world-wide Utopia, or face oblivion. This is an aside. The big issue is that there is, with the concept of more-with-lessing, potential abundance for all. Technology developed to its present conceivable ultimate would be capable of furnishing all of humanity not only with a comfortable life style, but with luxurious living. Competition is only necessary where there are scarcities, and in a highly technological world there is plenty for all and no scarcities, thus undermining the concept of survival of the fittest.

We will look at a theoretical society that is attainable with current trends in technology. The fact that it hasn't happened doesn't mean that it couldn't, nor that it won't. Technology develops at such a fast rate that what appears to be the science fiction of yesterday is the reality of today.

ECONOMY

Energy is supplied to each housing complex or center where people congregate, in a small nuclear package. It perhaps occasionally needs

---

[2] R. Buckminister Fuller, *Utopia or Oblivion: The Prospects for Humanity*, Chapter 9. Bantam Books, N.Y., 1969.

replacing or modification, but it is reliable and supplies all the power needed for one or more complexes, depending on size.

Materials and styles for housing and buildings have been so developed that full use may be made of natural resources, with malleable and easily handled units.

New food sources and food supplements have been developed so that cultivation of the land to grow food products is not necessary. Gourmet tastes may be satisfied with carefully cultivated food from a private garden, but this is engaged in as a hobby, rather than a necessity.

Water is attained either by private wells that are powered by the energy unit, or piped to different parts of each country from the salt water processing stations located in coastal regions throughout the world.

The division of labor is great, among those who labor. A new concept of work and leisure time is developed because nobody is in need of an income. There are plenty of material goods for all, and it is only those who desire to do so and/or who possess a much needed aptitude that are part of the labor force. There are many scientists following the concept of more-for-less in every conceivable area. These people have laboratories in their housing complex, maintain close-televised communication with each other and meet in groups for massive pooling of information.

Information and knowledge is stored in gigantic computers to which there is access at every local level that would require it. There is some need for computer maintenance although most of it is done by other than human resources.

Factories for production of consumer goods are strategically located throughout each country. When a household needs a specific item, a request is made (by computer) and the item is either manufactured or removed from storage (all done mechanically). It is then shipped to the requestor by whatever transportation system is currently in use, considering the distance. Portions of the transportation system are mechanized so that a person can request an item that arrives the following day and has no contact with humans.

Communication is immediate and reliable. Voice or visual projection are available to all individuals anywhere. Access to numerous taped programs of almost limitless variety is available at all times, as well as live output from information centers.

Health is an area that has had a great deal of study. Lifelong immunizations are made shortly after birth against the most destructive diseases. There are medical doctors in the society, but frequently the households are large enough to each contain one of their own. If a medium sized household is lacking an M.D., attempts will be made to socialize one of the young into gaining an education in that area.

Transportation is advanced. Each housing complex has as many private airborne vehicles as they desire, but the desire is not great. Most travel is to far away places and massive space or airliners are efficient in getting people to their destination. Resorts for visitors are located throughout the world, but communication is such that most people have made personal contact with individuals world-wide and visit in private housing complexes. There is a trend toward a universal language.

There are a few central air and space control centers. They develop and disseminate the special instructions concerning use of the atmosphere for transportation purposes. They keep constant tabs on what is going on and where, and dissipate potential air jams and emergencies of various sorts. Even the smallest air machine contains communication with the air and space centers.

Socialization of the young has been a crucial element in the transition of the industrial society to this post-post-industrial society. The concept and value of competition and laissez faire have been replaced with values and new concepts of leisure and cooperation. The positions that human beings fill in factories, computer centers, and other centers, for instance hospitals, are highly regarded and individuals must possess certain aptitudes to be accepted to fill them. Most of the education necessary to fill these roles is available in each housing complex. If accepted for a position, there are a variety of ways of handling it. Some people like to go to work every day. Others like to do most of it at home. Some people will work at their center for several days and then return home for several days of leisure. There is variation, depending on the individual and the type of work.

Socialization of differences between male and female diminishes. The female is as apt to become the medical doctor or the scientist or the air-space control technician as the male. The male is as apt to tend the children and take pride in gourmet cooking and gardening. This is more dependent upon aptitude than upon anything else.

With plenty of everything for all, a monetary system is not necessary as in the industrial competitive society. Collections might be made of rare items for a hobby, and occasional exchanges made between individuals, but this is an individual matter.

FAMILY

With no necessity for mobility, and rapid transportation when mobility is desired and required, there is general evolution from the small conjugal family to an extended family. The extended family is not necessarily a kinship group. It may consist entirely of non-blood relationships because of other bonds. Since housing facilities are simple and available, a housing complex may be as large or as small as desired. The smaller ones will rely on more outside institutions than the larger ones. The larger ones may be internally self-sufficient. Some couples may be attracted exclusively to each other for varying periods of time. A couple thus attracted might move from both of their respective housing complexes into a third complex where they are welcomed and where they feel comfortable. Or they may desire to begin their own private complex. . . .

EDUCATION

With the economy decentralized, all goods available to everyone, a division of labor that concerns only a small portion of the population, and large family units, the institution of education diminishes and most education and socialization is conducted in the housing complex. Learning machines are available, and it is only when someone's specialty and aptitude [are] quite unique that the learner goes outside of the housing complex for his education. . . .

SUMMARY

A lot of things have not been considered here. For instance, deviance. How will disruptive deviant behavior in a society of this kind be handled? Or will there be unacceptable behavior? Are there enough behavioral paths permitted that the concept of deviant behavior, especially in a negative sense, is no longer applicable? Another area, probably fitting under the heading of deviance, is mental health. The definitions of neurotic and psychotic will change as the value system changes.

One of the big problems any society like ours, with a competitive and monetary system has is the difficulty of accepting the notion that there is plenty for all, and that we can eliminate the excessively wealthy as well as those who now live in poverty. Another concept which would have to disappear is that everybody, to have self-fulfillment, needs to have an occupation. At this point the middle class and working class are at a disadvantage. Those at each end, with inherited wealth, and those living off of welfare or who can't get employment, are already more accepting of this philosophy and would have less difficulty accepting the technological Utopia, that is they would have less trouble socializing their children with the values of the new system, because it probably wouldn't come about overnight.

Perhaps this is an unrealistic approach to the search for Utopia, but is it any less realistic than turning one's back to the mechanization of the modern world and trying to dig a good life from the land by more primitive means? Would it not be more practical to begin seeking means to utilize the technology in order to achieve a more meaningful life? Some of the current uses will have to be rejected, but to reject technology because of the manner in which it is used seems a waste of knowledge. Nuclear energy can be used for purposes other than for bombs and destruction.

It is hard with our socialization and values (even though we frequently don't approve of them) to visualize a society such as the one postulated here. Our current trends would lead us to believe that the novel *1984* by George Orwell would more nearly represent our future. The novel *Island* by Aldous Huxley presents a lovely Utopia, but it realistically ends up being destroyed by other war-like people of the world. With the impact and strength of modern technology and weapons, it would appear that Fuller is right, it will be world-wide Utopia or oblivion.